JESUS CHRIST THE LORD

DR. J. STEPHEN

ISBN-10: 1479368660
ISBN-13: 978-1479368662

CONTENTS

Jesus Calls

(A Registered Charitable & Religious Trust)
16, Greenways Road, Chennai - 600 028, South India.

	Office	: 4958999
Ø	: Prayer Tower	: 4937722
Fax	: 91-44- 4936988, 4914911
Email	: dgs@prayertoweronline.org
	paul@prayertoweronline.org
Website	: www.prayertoweronline.org

Founders :
Dr. D.G.S. DHINAKARAN, C.A.I.I.B., Ph.D.
Dr. PAUL DHINAKARAN, M.B.A., Ph.D.

August 17, 2001

Foreword

The author, Dr. Stephen is well known to me for the past 25 years. I am really thrilled to have the honour of writing a foreword to this book, "Jesus Christ, the Lord". There is no dearth of books on various aspects of Christianity, now-a-days. But as I went through this book, I felt the difference just like 'a flower among vegetables' – this book stands unique since Jesus is the central theme of this book.

We are in the threshold of end times and everywhere we hear of wars and rumours of wars; nations rise against nations; famine, pestilence and earthquakes rock the world; people frantically run for a solution in vain. The solution lies in this book which directs mankind to find Jesus as one's personal Saviour and taste Him personally as the 'Lamb of God that takes away the sins of the world'. The author has succeeded in this attempt of wiping away the tears of the suffering humanity by presenting Jesus as the Lord who heals, who cares for all; as the revelation of the invisible God and the greatest love- gift of God for mankind.

The author's personal encounter with Jesus will prove as a challenge to every seeker. The prayer given at the end of each chapter will lead the seekers to commit themselves to our Lord Jesus and the believer will be led into deeper fellowship with his Saviour.

It is my fervent prayer that this book should lead every reader to respond to the compassionate call of our Lord Jesus "Come to Me all you who labour and are heavy laden, and I will give you rest".

May the Lord bless the author in his spiritual journey with deeper experiences and use him as a vessel of blessing to many.

D.G.S DHINAKARAN

THE AUTHOR'S NOTE

I thank and praise God Almighty and His only begotten Son Lord Jesus Christ of Nazareth for granting me the grace to write this book after several years of Bible learning and meditation. From the very outset let me state that I am neither qualified nor competent to write a book on the identity of our Lord and Saviour Jesus Christ. But it has been very painful to hear anyone deny the divinity of Jesus, or to realise that there are many who consider Him as one of several gods. Although I am only an ordinary man engaged in scientific research and teaching, it pleased my Lord to reveal Himself through the Word of God, through the sermons and writings of great men of God, and also through my own humble spiritual experiences, and thus I strongly feel that I must publish these facts, at the earliest, for the benefit of my fellow beings. I could not avoid profuse quotations from the Bible as I found my words rather inadequate to express the message contained in those passages. I have only compiled the evidences from the Bible itself to prove that Jesus Christ is the Lord. For authenticity, accuracy, and power, I have quoted only from King James' Version of the Bible.

With humble thanks unto the Lord, I remember all those who led me to true Christian faith, starting from my parents, Sunday School teachers, elders, pastors, missionaries, and preachers, up to great men of God from different nationalities. My sincere thanks are due to Rt.Revd Dr. Samuel Amirtham, former Bishop of CSI South Kerala Diocese, who had inducted me in the preaching ministry when he was the Presbyter of Abbs Memorial Church, Parassala. I am most grateful to my most beloved and esteemed Brother Dr. D.G.S. Dhinakaran, founder of Jesus Calls International Ministries, Madras, for his boundless love and concern for me and my family, and for his constant fervent prayers, guidance, advice, and encouragements. I have been greatly benefitted spiritually from his prayer festivals and Jesus Calls Institute of Power Ministry. I was also greatly privileged to have his prayerful foreword for this book, which he wrote despite his busy gospel activities. I am deeply indebted to Pastor L. Sam, a great preacher, Bible teacher, and famous interpreter from Trivandrum, for the introduction to the author. For their prayers and encouragements, I am thankful to the Most Revd.I.Jesudasan (former Moderator of the Church of South India, Trivandrum), Very Revd John Stott (former Rector of All Souls, London W1, where I was an active member in the 1970s), Bro.Oral Roberts (founder of Oral Roberts Ministries, Tulsa, USA), and Revd David Terrell (David Terrell Revivals, Texarcana, USA).

My hearty thanks are due to my beloved wife Pamela and my beloved children Ruth, Sam, and Sarah for their sincere cooperation and support. I am most thankful to Sarah for patiently revising and editing this book into its present form. Let me also thank all those who encourage me and uphold me in their prayers. With utmost humility and ardent devotion, I once again submit this book entitled 'JESUS CHRIST THE LORD' at the feet of my Lord and Saviour Jesus Christ as a humble tribute for the glory of God and for God's blessings upon the mankind.

Trivandrum,   J. Stephen

29th April, 2012.

"All things are delivered to me of my Father: and no man knoweth who the Son is but the Father; and who the Father is, but the Son, and he to whom the Son will reveal him",

Jesus in Luke 10:22

1

JESUS CHRIST - THE REVELATION OF THE INVISIBLE GOD

No man hath seen God at any time; the only begotten Son, which is in the bosom of the Father, he hath declared him

John 1:18

Archaeological findings demonstrates that, since prehistoric times, humans had been worshipping wonderful and magnificent objects of nature, such as sun, moon, earth, stars, comets, lightning and thunder, fire, wind, rivers, mountains, trees, and several animals and birds. Besides these, they used to worship several gods and goddesses who were probably either great men or women of ancient times, possessing extraordinary valour and charm, or characters born in the imaginative minds of great poets and epic writers. Even in the present millennium, several sects of communities and religions consider and worship their leaders as incarnations of certain deities. On the other hand, throughout many millennia, there lived great thinkers and sages who were in search of the supreme true God.

The Bible clearly proclaims that there is only one God. Of the ten commandments given by God to Moses at Mt. Sinai (also known as Mt. Horeb), the first and foremost commandment is: *I am the LORD thy God, which brought thee out of the land of Egypt, out of the house of bondage. Thou shalt have no other gods before me* (Exodus 20:23). On an earlier occasion (in Exodus 3: 2-4), at the same mountain, God appeared unto Moses in the midst of a burning bush, where irrespective of the raging fire, the bush was not consumed to ashes! When Moses approached the burning bush to solve the mystery, he heard a voice calling him by his name: *Moses, Moses*. The unseen voice continued: *Draw not nigh hither: Put off thy shoes from off thy feet, for the place where on thou standest is holy ground. I am the God of thy father, the God of Abraham, the God of Isaac and the God of Jacob* (Exodus 3: 5-6). Although God Himself was speaking to Moses face to face, the latter was unable to see the form of God except for the dazzling light and fire. Moses hid his face, for he was afraid to look upon God for truly none can stand before the glory of God. God is the God of glory and is a consuming fire. Moreover, God is the God of Adam, Enoch, Noah, Abraham, Isaac, Jacob, Joseph, Moses, Joshua, Samuel, David, Elijah, Elisha, Daniel, and prophets and saints of all times. He is the God of our forefathers, ours, and of our children from generation to generation, forever and ever.

When Moses asked for the name of God, He said unto Moses: *I AM THAT I AM* (Exodus 3:14). God is what God is. GOD is GOD; man is man. We cannot compare God with any person, being, spirit, matter, or energy. God is the most holy, supreme, omnipotent, omnipresent, omniscient, immortal, immutable, invisible, and supernatural person of "*highest wisdom and most radiant beauty*", as described by Albert Einstein[1].

Isaiah 40:12 states, *Who hath measured the waters in the hollow of his hand, and meted out heaven with the span, and comprehended the dust of the earth in a measure, and weighed the mountains in scales, and hills in a balance?* In verse 25 of the same chapter, God queries, *To whom then will ye liken me, or shall I be equal? saith the Holy One.* God is incomparable. If anyone compares God with earthly beings or pagan gods, the wrath of God will surely come upon him. This is explained in Romans 1:18-25, *For the wrath of God is revealed from heaven against all ungodliness and unrighteousness of men, who hold the truth in unrighteousness. Because that which may be known of God is manifest in them; for God hath shewed it unto them.*

[1] Einstein, Albert (1931). *Living Philosophies* (pp. 3-7) New York: Simon Schuster

For the invisible things of him from the creation of the world are clearly seen, being understood by the things that are made, even his eternal power and Godhead; so that they are without excuse: Because that, when they knew God, they glorified him not as God, neither were thankful; but became vain in their imaginations, and their foolish heart was darkened. Professing themselves to be wise, they became fools, And changed the glory of the uncorruptible God into an image made like to corruptible man, and to birds, and fourfooted beasts, and creeping things. Wherefore God also gave them up to uncleanness through the lusts of their own hearts, to dishonour their own bodies between themselves: Who changed the truth of God into a lie, and worshipped and served the creature more than the Creator, who is blessed for ever, Amen. This passage from St. Paul's epistle to the Romans explains why the vast majority of people around the world failed to recognise the true God and went astray to worship God's creations or gods of their own imaginations.

The Bible presents several encounters of God and His angels with people of different eras. Before sin entered the Garden of Eden, God was intimately associated with Adam and Eve, His own creations in His own form (Genesis 1:26). When they broke God's covenant (Genesis 3), God cursed them and drove them out of the garden. However, God continued to speak to their descendants. He spoke to their son Cain after he murdered his own brother Abel. In Genesis 5:22-24, we read of how Enoch walked with God, resulting in God taking him to heaven without him seeing death. God spoke to Noah (Genesis 6: 13-22) about his decision to destroy the wicked people of the earth by means of the great flood, and provides Noah with exact measurement of the ark which should house him and his family, and all fauna species of the world, during the great flood. In the above instances, it seems that God spoke to these individuals without appearing in His physical form.

Subsequently, we find that God spoke to Abraham on several occasions, and Abraham obeyed God implicitly. On one notable occasion (Genesis 18), assuming human form and concealing their true identities, God visited Abraham along with two angels. Abraham was very hospitable and received them into his tent assuming that they were travellers from a far-away land, and served the choicest meals for them. It was then God prophesised to Abraham, *Sarah thy wife shall have a so*n (Genesis 18:10). Later, He revealed, to Abraham, His plan to destroy the twin cities of Sodom and Gomorrah because of the abominations practiced by the inhabitants. After God *went his way,* the two angels went to Lot, Abraham's nephew, and rescued him and his family out of Sodom, before they destroyed the cities. In Genesis 32, Jacob wrestles with an angel and when he finally recognised the identity of his opponent, he insisted that the angel should bless him.

It was after more than 400 years that God revealed Himself to Moses in the midst of the burning bush at Mt. Horeb. After several months, God brought Moses and the children of Israel to the foothills of the same mountain, after God liberated them out of Egypt using numerous signs and wonders. When Moses went up the mountain to pray to God, he was asked to descend to the foothills and prepare the Israelites to meet God. I tremble upon reading or remembering the description of God's encounter with the children of Israel at Mt Sinai. This is how Exodus chapter 19 (verses 14-22) explains: *And Moses went down from the mount unto the people, and sanctified the people; and they washed their clothes. And he said unto the people, Be ready against the third day. Come not at your wives. And it came to pass on the third day in the morning, that there were thunders and lightnings, and a thick cloud upon the mount, and the voice of the trumpet exceeding loud; so that all the people that was in the camp trembled. And Moses brought forth the people out of the camp to meet with God; and they stood at the nether part of the mount. And mount Sinai was altogether on a smoke, because the LORD descended upon it in fire: and the smoke thereof ascended as the smoke of a furnace, and the whole mount quaked greatly. And when the voice of the trumpet sounded long, and waxed louder and louder, Moses spake, and God answered him by a voice. And the LORD came down upon mount Sinai, on the top of the mount: and the Lord called Moses up to the top of the mount: and Moses went up. And Lord said unto Moses, Go down, charge the people, lest they break through unto the LORD to gaze and many of them perish. And let the priests also, which come near to the LORD, sanctify themselves, lest the LORD break forth upon them.* God is most holy and the ground on which He descends becomes holy. Psalm 15:1-2 queries: *LORD, who shall abide in thy tabernacle? who shall dwell in thy holy hill? He that walketh uprightly, and worketh righteousness, and speaketh the truth in his heart.* In Leviticus 11:45 it is written: *For I am the LORD that bringeth you up out of Egypt, to be your God: ye shall therefore be holy, for I am holy.* The same essence is conveyed in I Peter 1:16.

Once, Moses greatly desired to see God. God pointed out that, *Thou canst not see my face: for there shall be no man see me, and live.*, and offers a solution: *Behold, there is a place by me, and thou shalt stand upon a rock: And it shall come to pass, while my glory passeth by, that I will put thee in a clift of the rock, and will cover thee with my hand while I pass by: And I will take away mine hand, and thou shalt see my back parts: but my face shall not be seen* (Exodus 33:20-23). Thus, Moses got only a visual glimpse of the glory of God's back, never seeing Him face-to-face, even though he was privileged to hear God's words, speak to Him, and feel His mighty presence.

God's presence was also in the most holy place of the tabernacle, where the ark of covenant was kept, and also in the cloudy pillar and pillar of fire which stood over the tabernacle during day and night respectively. In Exodus chapter 24 (verses 9-11), Moses, along with the elders of Israel, went up the mountain to meet God with the sacrificial blood of oxen slain on the altar. It is narrated as follows: *Then went up Moses, and Aaron, Nadab, and Abihu, and seventy of the elders of Israel: And they saw the God of Israel: and there was under his feet as it were a paved work of a sapphire stone, and as it were the body of heaven in his clearness. And upon the nobles of the children of Israel he laid not his hand: also they saw God, and did eat and drink.* Again, we can infer that they saw only part of the glory of God, and not His glorious form which no human eye can perceive and yet survive.

Joshua 5:13-15 portrays another incident: *And it came to pass, when Joshua was by Jericho, that he lifted up his eyes and looked, and behold, there stood a man over against him with his sword drawn in his hand: and Joshua went unto him, and said unto him, Art thou for us, or for our adversaries? And he said, Nay; but as captain of the host of the LORD am I now come. And Joshua fell on his face to the earth, and did worship, and said unto him, What saith my lord unto his servant? And the captain of the LORD's host said unto Joshua, Loose thy shoe from off thy foot; for the place whereon thou standest is holy. And Joshua did so.*

Upon going through the Bible, we come across several incidents in which angels of God appeared unto chosen men and women of God. They never allowed people to worship them, advising them to worship only God. Contrastingly, in the above incident, the Captain of LORD's host accepted Joshua's worship, and also commanded him to remove his shoes since that ground was holy. Hence the captain of LORD's host must had been be Jesus Christ himself, *the King of Kings, LORD of Lords, and LORD of hosts* (Revelation 19:11-16), who himself came to help the children of Israel in capturing the fort of Jericho. However, he appeared unto Joshua as the Chief Commander of God's army, setting aside his heavenly glory. In the book of Daniel 3: 25, when Shadrach, Meshach, and Abednego were bound and thrown into the fiery furnace because of their faith and testimony of the living true God, an astonished King Nebuchadnezzar exclaimed: *Lo, I see four men loose, walking in the midst of the fire, and they have no hurt; and the form of the fourth is like the Son of God.* Yes, he too saw Jesus Christ, the Son of God, who descended from heaven to the fiery furnace, to personally set free these men of God, and to convict Nebuchadnezzar of his arrogance and abominations. These two incidents serve as examples of the intervention of Jesus Christ, the Alpha and Omega, before he appeared in flesh and blood some two thousand years ago.

When King Belteshazzar, son of Nebuchadnezzar, hosted a great feast for his lords and concubines, and drank wine from the golden and silver vessels taken away from the temple of God in Jerusalem, he suddenly grew pale upon seeing a man's hand writing upon the wall - "*MENE, MENE, TEKEL, UPHARSIN*". The prophet Daniel pointed out that it was the hand of God Himself writing on the wall, and interpreted the cryptic words: *God hath numbered thy kingdom, and finished it. Thou art weighed in the balances, and art found wanting. Thy kingdom is divided, and given to the Medes and Persians* (Daniel 5:25-28). Belshazzar, the king of the Chaldeans, was slain that very night, and Darius, the Median king, took the kingdom. In the above incident, the wicked king who exalted himself could see the hand of God but not His face.

In Chapter 19 of the first book of Kings, God confronts His mighty prophet Elijah, who had fled to Mount Horeb to save his life when threatened by Queen Jezebel. God asked him, *What doest thou here, Elijah?* When he poured out his heart before the Lord, He said, *Go forth, and stand upon the mount before the Lord. And, behold, the LORD passed by, and a great and strong wind rent the mountains, and brake in pieces the rocks before the LORD; but the LORD was not in the wind: and after the wind an earth quake; but the LORD was not in the earthquake: And after the earthquake a fire; but the LORD was not in the fire: and after the fire a small still voice. And it was so, when Elijah heard it, that he wrapped his face in his mantle, and went out, and stood in the entering in of the cave. And behold there came a voice unto him, and said, What doest thou here, Elijah?* (I Kings 19:9;11-13). Here too Elijah heard God's voice, but could not see Him.

Great prophets such as Isaiah, Ezekiel, Daniel, and Zachariah had visions of God. But visions do not give the clarity of image as seen through open eyes, but as if seen through ground Although several people had encounters with the Almighty God, they could not see His form in the height of His heavenly glory, but could hear His voice and respond to His words, thus supporting the verse, *No man hath seen God at any time* (John 1:18). On the other hand, those who lived in the holy land two thousand years ago had the unique fortune to see God manifested in flesh and blood in the historic person of Jesus Christ. That was why Jesus told his disciples: *Blessed are the eyes which see the things that ye see: For I tell you, that many prophets and kings have desired to see those things which ye see, and have not seen them; and to hear those things which ye hear, and have not heard them* (Luke 10:23 & 24). The entire life of Jesus Christ was, in fact, the revelation of the invisible, omnipotent God. Truly he was the proverbial 'chip of the old block' – light from light, truth from truth, true God from true God, as proclaimed in the Nicene creed.

Jesus was gracious in his appearance, in his words, in his character, and in his ministry. He was the very embodiment of holiness, grace, truth, love, compassion, and all other noble virtues as the heavenly Father Himself. This was why Jesus said to his disciple Philip, who desired him to show him the heavenly Father: *Have I been so long time with you, and yet hast thou not known me, Philip? he that hath seen me hath seen the Father; and how sayest thou then, Shew us the Father? Believest thou not that I am in the Father, and the Father in me? the words that I speak unto you I speak not of myself: but the Father that dwelleth in me, he doeth the works. Believe me that I am in the Father, and the Father in me: or else believe me for the very works' sake* (John 14: 9-11).

In the gospel according to St. John, Lord Jesus reveals himself further in different contexts. Towards the end of the conversation between Jesus at the Samaritan woman at Jacob's Well, the woman says: *I know that Messias cometh, which is called Christ: when he is come, he will tell us all things. Jesus saith unto her, I that speak unto thee am he* (John 4:25-26). Once, to the multitude of people who were following him not to hear the gospel but to receive bread, Jesus said, *I am that bread of life.* (John 6:48). *I am the living bread which came down from heaven: if any man eat of this bread, he shall live for ever: and the bread that I will give is my flesh, which I will give for the life of the world* (John 6:51). The meaning of Jesus' words was not understood by the people, and the disciples and believers understood this only after the institution of Lord's Supper (Holy Communion).

On another occasion, Jesus tells the people who brought before him a woman caught in adultery: *He that is without sin among you, let him first cast a stone at her* (John 8:7). Convicted by their own conscience, the mob left the woman. Later Jesus declares unto them: *I am the light of the world: he that followeth me shall not walk in darkness, but shall have the light of life* (John 8:12). St. John writes in his first epistle: *This then is the message which we have heard of him* (Jesus), *and declare unto you, that God is light, and in him is no darkness at all* (I John 1:5). He writes in his gospel: *That was the true Light, which lighteth every man that cometh into the world* (John 1:9). John is referring to Jesus Christ who is the true Light from the true Light (God the Father) before whom every thing is revealed as such.

In another context, Jesus heals a man who was born blind, who was cast out from the synagogue by the Pharisees. When Jesus heard this, he found the blind man and asked, *Dost thou believe on the Son of God?* The blind man asked, *Who is he, Lord, that I might believe on him? And Jesus said unto him, Thou hast both seen him, and it is he that talketh with thee. And he said, Lord I believe. And he worshipped him* (John 9:35-38).

In John 10:11 Jesus says, *I am the good shepherd: the good shepherd giveth his life for the sheep.* He further says: *My sheep hear my voice, and I know them, and they follow me: And I give unto them eternal life: and they shall never perish, neither shall any man pluck them out of my hand. My Father, which gave them me, is greater than all; and no man is able to pluck them out of my Father's hand. I and my Father are one* (John 10:27-30). This made the Jews pick up stones to throw at Jesus whom they thought spoke blasphemy. Then Jesus said: *Say ye of him, whom the Father hath sanctified, and sent into the world, Thou blasphemest; because I said, I am the Son of God? If I do not the works of my Father, believe me not. But if I do, though ye believe not me, believe the works: that ye may know, and believe, that the Father is in me, and I in him* (John 10:36-38).

Four days after the death of their friend Lazarus, Jesus and his disciples went to Bethany and was met by Lazarus' sister Martha, who said to Jesus, *Lord, if thou hadst been here, my brother had not died. But I know, that even now, whatsoever thou wilt ask of God, God will give it thee. Jesus saith unto her, Thy brother shall rise again. Martha saith unto him, I know that he shall rise again in the resurrection at the last day. Jesus said unto her, I am the resurrection, and the life: he that believeth in me, though he were dead, yet shall he live: And whosoever liveth and believeth in me shall never die. Believest thou this?* (John 11:21-26). Lord Jesus went on to raise Lazarus, whose body was stinking four days after his death, and later proved that he is the resurrection and the life by his own resurrection.

The most important attribute of God is that He is immortal and eternal. Jesus took up death but, as per the Biblical prophecy in Psalm 16:10, his body did not undergo deterioration or corruption, and he rose again on the third day - not in the mortal human body subjected to natural laws, but in the heavenly body which could even pass through the closed door, unbound by natural laws. He triumphed over death and devil once for all. No power on earth, in hell, or in heaven can bind the resurrected Jesus. That was why Jesus declared unto his beloved disciple John who was exiled on the isle of

Patmos: *Fear not; I am the first and the last: I am he that liveth, and was dead; and, behold, I am alive for ever more, Amen; and have the keys of hell and of death* (Revelation 1:17 & 18). All men and women born on this earth are bound to die and become dust, with the exception of Enoch and Elijah (who were taken alive into heaven), and also the elect who will be translated upon Jesus' second coming. Those whom Jesus raised from the dead- the daughter of Jairus, the son of Nain's widow, and Lazarus- faced death later upon completion of their assigned ages. But Jesus lives forever and ever, proving beyond doubt that he is God, and we worship the risen Christ, who is glorified and exalted on the heavenly throne.

After Judas Iscariot left them after the last supper, Jesus admonished his remaining eleven disciples. He comforts them by saying that he goes to prepare a place for them and will come again afterwards to receive them. When Thomas stated that they were unaware of Jesus' destination and the way, Jesus replied: *I am the way, the truth, and the life: no man cometh unto the Father, but by me* (John 14:6). Yes, Jesus is the **only way** to the heavenly Father. Only through him, and only through his sacrificial blood, can we approach the heavenly throne of grace. Jesus is **the truth** -the ultimate truth, whom the sages sought through the ages. He is **the life** eternal and the most abundant life!

Jesus goes on to say: *I am the true vine, and my Father is the husbandman* (John 15:1). He repetitively points out: *I am the vine, ye are the branches: He that abideth in me, and I in him, the same bringeth forth much fruit: for without me ye can do nothing* (John 15.5). God had brought a vine from Egypt and planted it in the most sacred and fertile soil of Palestine. Contrary to His expectations, it gave forth wild grapes (Isaiah.5:1-4). It is by replacing this vine that God gave us the true vine- Jesus Christ- through whom emerged (and is still emerging) a new generation of God's children, bearing the characteristics of the good fruits. How wonderful is God's plan!

11

Lastly, in his heavenly glory, Jesus appeared to his most beloved disciple, St. John, in the island of Patmos to where he was exiled for preaching in the name of Jesus. In trumpet tongue, Jesus proclaims: *I am Alpha and Omega, the first and the last* (Revelation 1:11). Jesus uses the first and the last letters of the Greek alphabet (Alpha and Omega) to illustrate that he has been in existence with God the Father even before the foundation of the worlds (including heaven), and will be with Him forever. In other words, Jesus Christ is eternal and immortal, satisfying the greatest attribute of God. Once when confronted by the unbelieving Jews, Jesus said: *Your father Abraham rejoiced to see my day: and he saw it, and was glad. Then said the Jews unto him, Thou art not yet fifty years old, and hast thou seen Abraham? Jesus said unto them, Verily, verily, I say unto you, Before Abraham was, I am* (John 8:56-58). Jesus uses "I am" and not "I was", meaning that he is in existence even before the creation of heaven and the earth, and he is the co-creator with the Father, of Adam and of all men and women of all times, including Abraham. That is why Jesus is also called the "*Everlasting Father*" (Isaiah 9:6).

Jesus says in John 6:46: *Not that any man hath seen the Father, save he which is of God, he hath seen the Father*, in John 10:37-38: *If I do not the works of my Father, believe me not. But if I do, though ye believe not me, believe the works: that ye may know, and believe, that the Father is in me, and I in him*, and in John 12:45: *And he that seeth me seeth him that sent me.*

The subsequent chapters in this book provide more insights on the identity of Jesus Christ. For now, let me conclude this chapter with the words of St. Paul: *Now unto the King eternal, immortal, invisible, the only wise God, be honour and glory for ever and ever. Amen* (I Timothy 1:17).

Immortal, invisible, God only wise,
In light inaccessible hid from our eyes

12

Most blessed, most glorious, the Ancient of Days,
Almightily, victorious, Thy great name we praise
(Hymn No.34, Methodist Hymn Book[2])

He came down to earth from heaven,
Who is God and Lord of all,
And His shelter was a stable,
And His cradle was a stall
With the poor, and mean and lowly
Lived on earth our Saviour holy
(Hymn No. 859, Methodist Hymn Book)

Could we join in prayer for a moment?

Lord Jesus Christ, God incarnate, Immanuel, Alpha and Omega, We come to thy holy presence with open minds. Reveal thyself to us better and better. Enable us to believe thee absolutely in child like faith and accept thee as our Lord and Saviour. Open our minds to understand thy wisdom; Open our hearts to understand thy love, open our eyes to see thy glory; open our ears to hear thy word and open our mouths to sing thy praise. Come into our hearts and dwell therein; teach us thy word as thou didst teach thy disciples; fill us with all thy noble qualities and Holy Spirit; help us to be thy mighty witnesses. In thy sweetest name we pray, Lord Jesus, and receive these blessings by faith. Amen.

---

[2] The Methodist Hymn Book 1933. London: John Wesley Publishing House

2

JESUS CHRIST-THE SON OF GOD, THE WORD MANIFESTED IN FLESH

And the Word was made flesh, and dwelt among us, (and we beheld his glory, the glory as of the only begotten of the Father,) full of grace and truth

John 1:14

The gospel according to St.John is unique in its presentation of our Lord and Saviour Jesus Christ as the Son of God and the Word manifested in flesh. Equivalent to the opening verse in the Bible, *In the beginning God created the heaven and the earth* (Genesis 1:1), St.John begins the gospel account by stating, *In the beginning was the Word, and the Word was with God, and the Word was God* (John 1:1). In fact, St.John is giving us a glimpse of the time long before God created the heaven, the earth, and His angels, when the Word – the Son of God, Jesus Christ- was with God. Merriam-Webster's dictionary[3] defines the term "word" (Gk.*logos*) as "a sound or combination of sounds that has a meaning and is spoken or written", with other definitions being "logos", "gospel", and "the expressed or manifested mind and will of God". But since only sounds which make a sense or meaning constitute a word, why is Jesus referred to as *the Word*? I believe that it is because Jesus Christ is the message from God to man – a message conveyed through his words and deeds. Jesus is God's word manifested in flesh. His life itself was the message of God's matchless love, compassion, forgiveness, redemption, grace, power, holiness, and glory. That is why St.John writes: *And the Word was made flesh, and dwelt among us (and we beheld his glory, the glory as of the only begotten of the Father), full of grace and truth* (John 1:14).

---

[3] Merriam-Webster Dictionary weblink: http://www.merriam-webster.com/dictionary/word?show=0&t=1397831657

In his first epistle, St.John writes: *That which was from the beginning, which we have heard, which we have seen with our eyes, which we have looked upon, and our hands have handled, of the Word of life; (For the life was manifested, and we have seen it, and bear witness, and shew unto you that eternal life, which was with the Father, and was manifested unto us;) That which we have seen and heard declare we unto you, that ye also may have fellowship with us; and truly our fellowship is with the Father, and with his Son Jesus Christ* (I John 1:1-3). St.John is referring to Jesus Christ, the Son of God, who dwelt among them, taught them the great mysteries of the kingdom of God, and, by adoption, converted them into the children of God. Truly, John was the disciple whom Jesus loved most and who followed him even unto his sacrificial death on the cross. John gives the most accurate eyewitness account of the life, teachings, and ministry of Jesus Christ. First of all, he declares to the world that Jesus is the Word of God, who was with God in eternal existence even before the foundation of heaven and earth. Secondly, he states that the Word (Jesus) **was and is** God. Thirdly, he states: *All things were made by him; and without him was not anything made that was made* (John 1:3). In Genesis 1:26, we read that *God said, Let us make man in our image, after our likeness: and let them have dominion over the fish of the sea, and over the fowl of the air, and over the cattle, and over all the earth, and over creeping thing that creepeth upon the earth.* From this we understand that God the Father was consulting with His Son, Jesus Christ, during the creation.

In his epistle to Colossians, St.Paul writes: *For by him were all things created, that are in heaven, and that are in earth, visible and invisible, whether they be thrones, or dominions, or principalities, or powers: all things were created by him, and for him: And he is before all things, and by him all things consist* (Colossians 1:16-17). Even before the invention of microscopes, telescopes, and other devices to detect invisible objects and rays, the Holy Spirit was revealing through St. Paul that there are also invisible matters and powers of material and spiritual worlds. Moreover, the above verse implies that the entire universe, and even the heaven, exist because of Jesus Christ, the Lord. He binds all things together in perfect harmony starting from subatomic particles up to the endless universe. In Psalm 2:7, God the Father refers to the time much before the creation of the heaven and the earth when He declares to His son Jesus Christ: *Thou art my Son; this day have I begotten thee*. The epistle to Hebrews begins thus: *God, who at sundry times and in divers manners spake in time past unto the fathers by the prophets, Hath in last days spoken unto us by His Son, whom he hath appointed heir of all things, by whom also he made the worlds; Who being the brightness of his glory, and the express image of his person, and upholding all things by the word of his power, when he had by himself purged our sins, sat down on the right hand of the Majesty on high; Being made so much better than the angels, as he hath by inheritance obtained a more excellent name than they. For unto which of the angels said he at any time, Thou art my Son, this day have I begotten thee? And again, I will be to him a Father, and he shall be to me a Son? And again, when he bringeth in the first begotten into the world, he saith, And let all the angels of God worship him. And of the angels he saith, Who maketh his angels spirits, and his ministers a flame of fire. But unto the Son he saith, Thy throne, O God, is for ever and ever: a sceptre of righteousness is the sceptre of thy kingdom. Thou hast loved righteousness, and hated iniquity; therefore God, even thy God, hath anointed thee with the oil of gladness above thy fellows. And, Thou, Lord, in the beginning hast laid the foundation of the earth; and the heavens are the works of thine hands: They shall perish; but thou remainest; and they all shall wax old as doth a garment; And as a vesture shalt thou fold them up, and they shall be changed: but thou art the same, and thy years shall not fail. But to which of the angels said he at any time, Sit on my right hand, until I make thine enemies thy footstool?* (Hebrews 1:1-13). These verses are all cited from the Old Testament of the Bible (Psalm 2:7, Psalm 104:4, Psalm 45:6-7, Isaiah 61:1 & 3, Psalm102: 25-27, and Psalm 110:1). The above passages clearly state that Jesus Christ has been with God the Father from infinite time, and not only is he the Saviour of the mankind, but also the Creator, Protector and the Ruler of the entire universe along with his heavenly Father.

In the book of Revelation chapter 19, St.John describes his vision of Jesus majestically riding on a white horse and leading his heavenly hosts. Let me quote it as such: *And I saw heaven opened, and behold a white horse; and he that sat upon him was called Faithful and True, and in righteousness he doth judge and make war. His eyes were as a flame of fire, and on his head were many crowns; and he had a name written, that no man knew, but he himself. And he was clothed with a vesture dipped in blood: and his name is called The Word of God. And the armies which were in heaven followed him upon white horses, clothed in fine linen, white and clean. And out of his mouth goeth a sharp sword, that with it he should smite the nations: and he shall rule them with a rod of iron: and he treadeth the winepress of the fierceness and wrath of Almighty God. And he hath on his vesture and on his thigh a name written, "KING OF KINGS, AND LORD OF LORDS"* (Revelation 19:11-16). All these verses clearly show that Jesus Christ is the Word of God, the Lord of heavenly hosts, the King of Kings, and Lord of Lords.

In Philippians 2:5-11, it is written: *Let this mind be in you, which was also in Christ Jesus: Who, being in the form of God, thought it not robbery to be equal with God: But made himself of no reputation, and took upon him the form of a servant, and was made in the likeness of men: And being found in fashion as a man, he humbled himself, and became obedient unto death, even the death of the cross. Wherefore God also hath highly exalted him, and given him a name which is above every name: That at the name of Jesus every knee should bow, of things in heaven, and things in earth, and things under the earth; and that every tongue should confess that Jesus Christ is Lord, to the glory of God the Father.* As written in Psalm 110:1, God the Father is telling Jesus Christ to sit on His right hand until He makes all his enemies his footstool. When the high priest asked Jesus whether he was the Christ, the Son of God, *Jesus said I am: and ye shall see the Son of man sitting on the right hand of power, and coming in the clouds of heaven* (Mark 14:62). In Luke's gospel, it is recorded as follows: *Hereafter shall the Son of man sit on the right hand of the power of God* (Luke 22:69). When the first Christian martyr,

St.Stephen, was being stoned to death by the fanatic Jews under the instigation of the high priest, he, being full of the Holy Spirit, looked up steadfastly into heaven and saw the glory of God and Jesus standing on the right hand of God. He cried out, *Behold, I see the heavens opened, and the Son of man standing on the right hand of God* (Acts 7:56). Several saints of God have had the same glorious vision when they died as martyrs during the first century AD and thereafter throughout all ages.

Several centuries before the earthly birth of Jesus Christ, Isaiah prophesied: *Therefore the Lord himself shall give you a sign; Behold, a virgin shall conceive, and bear a son and shall call his name Immanuel* (Isaiah7:14). *For unto us a child is born, unto us a son is given: and the government shall be upon his shoulder: and his name shall be called Wonderful, Counsellor, The mighty God, The everlasting Father, The Prince of Peace. Of the increase of his government, and peace there shall be no end, upon the throne of David, and upon his kingdom, to order it, and to establish it with judgment and with justice from henceforth even for ever. The zeal of the Lord of hosts will perform this* (Isaiah 9: 6- 7). Further, in Isaiah 11:1-2 it is written: *And there shall come forth a rod out of the stem of Jesse, and a Branch shall grow out of his roots: And the spirit of the Lord shall rest upon him, the spirit of wisdom and understanding, the spirit of counsel and might, the spirit of knowledge and of the fear of the Lord.* Even the place of his birth was foretold by Micah, the prophet: *But thou, Beth-lehem Ephratah, though thou be little among the thousands of Judah, yet out of thee shall he come forth unto me that is to be the ruler in Israel; whose goings forth have been from of old, from everlasting* (Micah 5:2). Thus, according to Old Testament prophesies, Jesus was conceived of the Holy Spirit and born of Virgin Mary into the race of Jesse and David in Bethlehem, the city of David, in conformity with the gospel accounts of St.Matthew and St.Luke. We read in Hebrews 2:14-16, *Forasmuch then as the children are partakers of flesh and blood, he also himself likewise took part of the same; that through death he might destroy him that had the power of death, that is, the devil; And deliver them who through fear of death were all their lifetime subject to bondage. For verily he took not on him the nature of angels; but he took on him the seed of Abraham.*

When the archangel Gabriel visited the virgin Mary to announce the good news that God had chosen her to give birth to the Son of God in flesh and blood, he said: *Fear not, Mary: for thou hast found favour with God. And, behold, thou shalt conceive in thy womb, and bring forth a son, and shalt call his name JESUS. He shall be great, and shall be called the Son of the Highest: and the Lord God shall give unto him the throne of his father David: And he shall reign over the house of Jacob for ever; and of his kingdom there shall be no end* (Luke 1:30-33). When Mary asked Gabriel how this could happen since she was a virgin, the archangel replied: *The Holy Ghost shall come upon thee, and the power of the Highest shall overshadow thee: therefore also that holy thing which shall be born of thee shall be called the Son of God. And, behold, thy cousin Elizabeth, she hath also conceived a son in her old age: and this is the sixth month with her, who was called barren. For with God nothing shall be impossible. And Mary said, Behold the handmaid of the Lord; be it unto me according to thy word. And the angel departed from her* (Luke 1:35-38).

Mary went hastily to meet her cousin Elizabeth, in whose womb the babe leaped when she heard the salutation of Mary. Filled with the Holy Spirit, Elizabeth spoke in a loud voice: *Blessed art thou among woman, and blessed is the fruit of thy womb. And whence is this to me, that the mother of my Lord should come to me? For, lo, as soon as the voice of thy salutation sounded in mine ears, the babe leaped in my womb for joy. And blessed is she that believed: for there shall be a performance of those things which were told her from the Lord* (Luke 1: 42-45). The above words were not from the brain of Elizabeth, but from the Holy Spirit, the Spirit of Truth. On hearing these words, Mary was also filled with the Holy Spirit and spoke the words known as the "Magnificat" (Luke 1:46-55). In the meantime, the angel of the Lord appeared in a dream to Joseph, who was espoused to Mary, saying: *Joseph, thou son of David, fear not to take unto thee Mary thy wife: for that which is conceived in her is of the Holy Ghost.*

And she shall bring forth a son, and thou shalt call his name JESUS: for he shall save his people from their sins. Now all this was done, that it might be fulfilled which was spoken of the Lord by the prophet saying, Behold, a virgin shall be with child, and shall bring forth a son, and they shall call his name Emmanuel, which being interpreted is, God with us. Then Joseph being raised from sleep did as the angel of the Lord had bidden him, and took unto him his wife: And knew her not till she had brought forth her firstborn son: and he called his name JESUS (Matthew 1: 20-25).

When Jesus was born in Bethlehem, of Judaea, there were shepherds, in the fields situated in the outskirts of the town, keeping watch over their flock by night. All of a sudden, an angel of the Lord came upon them and the glory of the Lord shone around. They were sore afraid, but the angel calmed them saying, *Fear not: for, behold, I bring you good tidings of great joy, which shall be to all people. For unto you is born this day in the city of David a Saviour, which is Christ the Lord. And this shall be a sign unto you; Ye shall find the babe wrapped in swaddling clothes, lying in a manger. And suddenly there was with the angel a multitude of the heavenly host praising God, and saying, Glory to God in the highest, and on earth peace, good will toward men* (Luke 2: 10-14). St. Luke further writes: *And it came to pass, as the angels were gone away from them into heaven, the shepherds said one to another, Let us now go even unto Bethlehem, and see this thing which is come to pass, which the Lord hath made known unto us. And they came with haste, and found Mary, and Joseph, and the babe lying in a manger. And when they had seen it, they made known abroad the saying which was told them concerning this child. And all they that heard it wondered at those things which were told them by the shepherds. But Mary kept all these things, and pondered them in her heart. And the shepherds returned, glorifying and praising God for all things that they had heard and seen, as it was told unto them* (Luke 2: 15-20). What a wonderful privilege the illiterate and innocent shepherds had! First of all, they heard the good news of the birth of Jesus Christ directly from the angel– perhaps it was an archangel of the Lord! They saw and heard the angelic choir singing the first carol. Above all, they were the first mortals to see and worship the newborn Saviour, and also to narrate all that they saw, and heard, concerning the child.

In the 2nd chapter of the gospel according to St.Matthew, we read about the visit of wise men from the East who queried: *Where is he that is born King of the Jews? for we have seen his star in the east, and are come to worship him* (Matthew 2:2). After reasoning that the King of the Jews should be born in the royal palace, they went directly to Jerusalem and met King Herod, who, with all Jerusalem, was troubled when they heard this news. Herod gathered all chief priests and scholars, and demanded to know where Christ should be born. The answer was in the prophecy of Micah, who predicted that Christ will be born in Bethlehem (Micah 5:2; Matthew 2:6). Then Herod, determined to kill the child who might become a threat to his reign if permitted to live, cunningly told the wise men to search diligently for the newborn king in Bethlehem, and to inform him upon finding the child, so that he too can worship him.

Following the directions, the wise men went to Bethlehem. The star, which had brought them to Jerusalem, went before them until it stood over where the young child was. *And when they were come into the house, they saw the young child with Mary his mother, and fell down, and worshipped him: and when they had opened their treasures, they presented unto him gifts; gold, and frankincense, and myrrh* (Matthew 2:11). Note that these learned wise men of far-away lands fell down before infant Jesus, recognised his divinity, worshipped him, and offered unto him, in a prophetic manner, gold (a presentation for the king), frankincense (to worship the Lord and God), and myrrh (a presentation to the Saviour of the cross). Yet, it was their intellectual reasoning which first led them astray to King Herod, subsequently resulting in the Massacre of the Innocents (children below the age of two) in Bethlehem and surrounding areas. On the other hand, the illiterate and innocent shepherds made no mistake and came directly to the manger where Jesus was born. The shepherds' actions represent the path of child-like faith, whereas the wise men's *modus operandi* represents the path of reasoning and Science.

When the infant Jesus was taken to the Temple of Jerusalem, to be dedicated holy unto the Lord, he was taken up in the arms of Simeon, a pious man of Jerusalem, who had come to the temple led by the Holy Spirit. St. Luke describes Simeon as follows: *and the same man was just and devout, waiting for the consolation of Israel: and the Holy Ghost was upon him. And it was revealed unto him by the Holy Ghost, that he should not see death, before he had seen the Lord's Christ* (Luke 2:25-26). Thus, Simeon could recognise the infant Jesus as the Messiah and Christ. He also prophesied, in the Holy Spirit, that this baby is the light to lighten the gentiles and the glory of God's people, the Israelites. He praised God saying: *Lord, now lettest thou thy servant depart in peace, according to thy word: For mine eyes have seen thy salvation, which thou hast prepared before the face of all people; A light to lighten the Gentiles, and the glory of thy people Israel* (Luke 2:29-32). Joseph and Mary marvelled at these utterances and Simeon blessed them, saying unto Mary, *Behold, this child is set for the fall and rising again of many in Israel; and for a sign which shall be spoken against: (Yea, a sword shall pierce through thy own soul also,) that the thoughts of many hearts may be revealed* (Luke 2:34-35). These statements are prophetic, indicating the gruesome crucifixion of Jesus, by which a sword would pierce through St Mary's heart, for it will be a heart-breaking experience. Anna, a prophetess who always stayed in the Temple, fasting and praying day and night, came and thanked God for the gift of this divine child, speaking of him to all who looked for the redemption in Jerusalem.

After twelve years, Jesus is left, unaware, in the Temple of Jerusalem, when Mary and Joseph had taken him for the Feast of Passover. It was only after three days that they found him sitting in the Temple of Jerusalem, *in the midst of the doctors, both hearing them, and asking them questions. And all that heard him were astonished at his understanding and answers* (Luke 2:46-47). Mary asked him, *Son, why hast thou thus dealt with us? behold, thy father and I have sought thee sorrowing. And he said unto them, How is it that ye sought me? wist ye not that must be about my Father's business?* (Luke 2:49). Yes, Jesus was doing the business of his Father, God Almighty Himself! But Mary and Joseph could not understand this. Even many years later, during the public ministry of Jesus, Mary came to take Jesus away with her. But he was determined to do the mission entrusted with him by God.

At the age of thirty, when Jesus went to John the Baptist, for being baptised by him in the river Jordan, John forbade him saying, *I have need to be baptized of thee, and comest thou to me? And Jesus answering said unto him, Suffer it to be so now: for thus it becometh us to fulfil all righteousness. Then he suffered him. And Jesus, when he was baptized, went up straightway out of the water: and, lo, the heavens were opened unto him, and he saw the Spirit of God descending like a dove, and lighting upon him: And lo a voice from heaven, saying, This is my beloved Son, in whom I am well pleased* (Matthew 3:13-17). John the Baptist bare record saying, *I saw the Spirit descending from heaven like a dove, and it abode upon him. And I knew him not: but he that sent me to baptize with water, the same said unto me, Upon whom thou shalt see the Spirit descending, and remaining on him, the same is he which baptizeth with the Holy Ghost* (John 1:32-34). Above all, God the Father Himself testified, *This is my beloved Son, in whom I am well pleased* (Matthew 3:17). God also spoke to the three great disciples of Jesus – Peter, James and John - on the Mount of Transfiguration: *This is my beloved Son, in whom I am well pleased; hear ye him* (Matthew 17:5). This is why St.John writes: *and we beheld his glory, the glory as of the only begotten of the Father* (John 1:14).

On the coasts of Caesarea Philippi, Jesus asked his disciples, *Whom do men say that I the Son of man am? And they said, Some say that thou art John the Baptist: some, Elias; and others, Jeremias, or one of the prophets. He saith unto them, But whom say ye that I am? And Simon Peter answered and said,*

Thou art the Christ, the Son of the living God. And Jesus answered and said unto him, Blessed art thou, Simon Bar-jona: for flesh and blood hath not revealed it unto thee, but my Father which is in heaven (Matthew 16:13-17). Jesus had already told his disciples, *All things are delivered unto me of my Father: and no man knoweth the Son, but the Father; neither knoweth any man the Father, save the Son, and he to whomsoever the Son will reveal him* (Matthew 11:27).

Even demons recognised Jesus, as seen at the synagogue at Capernaum, where a man possessed with an evil spirit cried out: *Let us alone; what have we to do with thee, thou Jesus of Nazareth? art thou come to destroy us? I know thee who thou art, the Holy One of God* (Mark 1:23-24). When Jesus was seen afar off, the man on the shore of Gadarenes (who was possessed by a legion of demons inciting him to live a miserable life of self-mutilation and self-tormentation) ran towards him and worshipped him. He cried out with a loud voice saying, *What have I to do with thee Jesus, thou Son of the most high God? I adjure thee by God, that thou torment me not* (Mark 5: 1-8). There are many more instances in which evil spirits recognised Jesus, calling out his name, and leaving the possessed people instantaneously.

The supernatural miracles, which Jesus did during the course of his public ministry, also firmly declare that he is the Son of God. After hearing Jesus' gracious words on the cross and after seeing the three-hour long complete darkness at noon, the earthquake, and other supernatural events, and the manner in which Jesus gave his life in the hands of his heavenly Father, the centurion who was in charge of Lord's crucifixion testified: *Truly this man was the Son of God* (Mark 15:39).

St.John writes in his gospel: *For he whom God hath sent speaketh the words of God: for God giveth not the Spirit by measure unto him. The Father loveth the Son, and hath given all things into his hand. He that believeth on the Son hath everlasting life: and he that believeth not the Son shall not see life; but the wrath of God abideth on him* (John 3:34-36). He writes in his second epistle: *Grace be with you, mercy, and peace from God the Father, and from the Lord Jesus Christ, the Son of the Father, in truth and love... For many deceivers are entered into the world, who confess not that Jesus Christ is come in the flesh. This is a deceiver and an antichrist. Look to yourselves, that we lose not those things which we have wrought, but that we receive a full reward. Whosoever transgresseth, and abideth not in the doctrine of Christ, hath not God. He that abideth in the doctrine of Christ, he hath both the Father and the Son. If there come any unto you, and bring not this doctrine, receive him not into your house, neither bid him God speed: For he that biddeth him God speed is partaker of his evil deeds* (II John 3, 7-11). In John 5:22-24, to the Jews who argue with him, Jesus says, *For the Father judgeth no man, but hath committed all judgment unto the Son: That all men should honour the Son, even as they honour the Father. He that honoureth not the Son honoureth not the Father which hath sent him. Verily, verily, I say unto you, He that heareth my word, and believeth on him that sent me, hath everlasting life, and shall not come into condemnation; but is passed from death unto life.* While explaining that he is the good shepherd who gives up his life for the sheep, Jesus says: *My sheep hear my voice, and I know them, and they follow me: And I give them eternal life; and they shall never perish, neither shall any man pluck them out of my hand. My Father, which gave them me, is greater than all; and no man is able to pluck them out of my Father's hand. I and my Father are one* (John 10:27-30).

Anyone's logical question would be: How can the Father and the Son be one? This is difficult to explain in human terms, and St Augustine was one among the many who were baffled by this question despite spending hours thinking[4]. One day, in a vision, he saw himself racking his brains in a seashore over the same question. Then, he observed a little boy industriously collecting the seawater in a large seashell and pouring it on a sand dune. St Augustine was amazed upon realising that the boy was doing this activity for a long time, and

---

[4] http://www.catholic-forum.com/saints/golden259.htm

he asked him what he was up to. The boy replied that he was drying up the sea by this process. Upon hearing this, St.Augustine burst into laughter and told him that he was very foolish. Immediately, to St. Augustine's surprise, the boy replied, "If I am so foolish, you are much more foolish. You are trying to understand the mystery of Godhead using your tiny brain. It is beyond your rational thinking and comprehension. You simply believe in the word of God." Suddenly the boy vanished. Then only did St.Augustine realise that the boy was none other than an angel of God sent to teach him this lesson.

I had read several books written by great authors on the doctrine of Holy Trinity - that the Father, the Son, and the Holy Spirit are three persons in one. Yet, I failed to comprehend the doctrine and various viewpoints. My discussions with several Biblical scholars failed to convince me. Eventually, I was in such a state that the mystery of the Holy Trinity was being constantly pondered upon. One day, I visited Mrs.Rajamma Ponnuswamy, a pious Christian lady of Neyyoor, for prayers. Without my asking her anything, she brought a bean leaf from her garden and asked me the number of leaves in that material. As a confident botanist, I responded, "Only one". Then pointing to the three leaflets in that leaf, she asked me, "Then, what are these?." I replied, "These are leaflets." She further queried, "Why do you say that these are leaflets and not independent leaves?." I patiently explained, "These three leaflets have a common leafstalk. Hence, they are leaflets and not leaves." She continued, "You have answered well. But how long have you been asking yourself how can the Father, the Son and the Holy Spirit be one? It was Jesus who asked me to show you this example." Greatly moved, I asked my gracious Lord Jesus to forgive my foolish rational thinking. This example of a bean leaf also provided a fascinating glimpse into the mind of Jesus. For me, whose primary specialisation is in Botany, he taught me a lesson from that subject so that it would be appealing to my understanding. Several years later, I read the testimony of an Oxford physicist to whom the

Lord gave an example of the sun, which was formed by the combination of the matter, light, and heat. These examples show that the Father, the Son, and the Holy Spirit are one in love, one in unity, one in eternity, one in character, and one in action. The Father always glorifies the Son; the Son always glorifies the Father; the Holy Spirit glorifies both the Father and the Son and enables the children of God to understand the Word of God in the correct sense and spirit, to worship the Father and the Son in truth and in spirit, and to be mighty witnesses for God.

Historically, during the Old Testament period, without revealing Himself in bodily form, God the Father spoke to Noah, Abraham, Moses, Joshua, and several prophets to give instructions, correction, and reproof to the chosen people. During the gospel time, Jesus, the Son of God, born in flesh and blood, dwelt among the people, showed them the way of salvation and life, explained the mysteries of the kingdom of God, healed the sick and broken hearted, delivered the demon-possessed, and raised them who died untimely. He revealed the love, compassion, and forgiveness of the heavenly Father not only through his teachings and ministry, but also through his supreme sacrifice on the cross and by redeeming mankind from the bondage of sin and the devil, so that they would become the children of the living Almighty God. From the Apostolic times until the second coming of Jesus Christ, the Holy Spirit dwells in the hearts of the believers, and also in the Church, providing deeper revelations about the Father and the Son, as well as the Word of God, so that believers will be motivated to spread the gospel around the world for the building up the body of Christ and to purify and sanctify the Church so as to make her the bride of Jesus Christ.

Glory be to God on high
And peace on earth descend:
God comes down, He bows the sky
And shows Himself our Friend:

God the invisible appears:
God, the blest, the great I AM,
Sojourns in this vale of tears,
And Jesus is His name.
(Hymn No: 134, Methodist Hymn Book[5])

1. Oh, wondrous Name, by prophets heard,
Long years before His birth;
They saw his coming from afar,
The Prince of Peace on earth,

The wonderful! The Counsellor
The Great and Mighty Lord!
The Everlasting Prince of Peace!
The King, the Son of God!

2. Oh, glorious Name, the angels praise,
And ransomed saints above -
The Name above all other names,
Our Refuge evermore.
3. Oh, precious Name, exalted high,
To whom all power is given,
Through Him we triumph over sin,
By him we enter heaven.
(Hymn No: 96, Sacred Songs & Solos[6])

Shall we join in the following prayer?

Loving Lord Jesus, Son of the Almighty God,

In humble adoration we come to thy holy presence with praises and thanksgiving. Words are inadequate to express our gratitude towards thee. Thou didst leave thy heavenly throne and God's bosom and came down to save us sinners who were doomed for eternal damnation. Thou taught us the secrets of the kingdom of God and by thy boundless love and grace granted

---

[5] The Methodist Hymn Book. London: John Wesley Publishing House, 1933

[6] Sankey, I. Sacred Songs and Solos. London: Marshall, Morgan, and Scott, 1981.

unto us the heavenly privileges. Now Lord, help us to understand thee more and more; help us to have a closer walk with thee day by day; help us to have communion with thee more and more; and help us to follow thy footsteps closer and closer. For thou art the way, the truth, and the life. Grant us thy abundant life; grant us thy fruits so that everyone who sees us will glorify thee. Help us to proclaim thy gospel far and near. Jesus, in thy most precious name we pray, Amen

3

JESUS CHRIST- GOD'S GREATEST GIFT OF LOVE FOR THE MANKIND

For God so loved the world, that he gave his only begotten Son, that whosoever believeth in him should not perish, but have everlasting life.

John 3:16

During the early days of Jesus' ministry in the Holy Land, he was visited by Nicodemus, a wise scholar and a Pharisee. This visit to felicitate Jesus' wonderful ministry among the sick and the suffering was undertaken at night since Nicodemus was reluctant to meet him in the broad daylight, fearing that the Jews might cast him out from the high positions and privileges which he had been enjoying. Yet, he wanted to secretly acknowledge Jesus as a Rabbi and as a prophet and receive blessings from him. Nicodemus said: *Rabbi, we know that thou art a teacher come from God: for no man can do these miracles that thou doest, except God be with him* (John 3:2). But Jesus said unto him, *Verily, verily, I say unto thee, Except a man be born again, he cannot see the kingdom of God* (John 3:3). Nicodemus obviously found this strange, for he asks Jesus, *How can a man be born when he is old? can he enter the second time into his mother's womb, and be born?* (John 3:4).

The *Maharajahs* (kings) of a South Indian state used to practise an unique religious ceremony for several centuries. Amidst the chanting of *vedas* by the priests, the *Maharaja* entered into the mouth of a huge silver effigy of a sacred cow, crawled through its belly, and emerged out through a giant hole at the posterior end. It was believed that this ceremony cleansed him from his past sins and that he was born again as a new creature. Jesus never meant this and clarifies this to Nicodemus, *Verily, verily I say unto thee, Except a man be born of water and*

30

of the Spirit, he cannot enter into the kingdom of God. That which is born of the flesh is flesh; and that which is born of the Spirit is spirit (John 3:5-6). Jesus provides more explanations on how to be born again. Many religions believe that should a man is unable to attain perfection and salvation in one lifecycle, and hence he will, after his first death, have rebirths assuming the form of some animal, and the process will be repeated until he becomes completely perfect in his deeds. The Bible clearly proclaims that there is only one life and that man will be judged according to his deeds in this life: *And as it is appointed unto men once to die, but after this the judgment* (Hebrews 9:27). Jesus tells Nicodemus, *And as Moses lifted up the serpent in the wilderness, even so must the Son of man be lifted up: That whosoever believeth in him should not perish, but have eternal life. For God so loved the world, that he gave his only begotten Son, that whosoever believeth in him should not perish, but have everlasting life* (John 3:14-16).

Jesus was reminding Nicodemus of a decisive episode during the exodus of the Israelites from the land of Egypt, as recorded in Numbers 21. They had journeyed from mount Hor, by the way of the Red Sea, to encircle the land of Edom. However, they were constantly grumbling and quarrelling against Moses, although God was miraculously leading them all the way long. After observing their repeated disobedience, God's anger was kindled and He sent fiery serpents which bit many of them, resulting in many deaths. Then the trembling Israelites came to Moses and repented of their transgressions and pleaded that he should request God to remove the serpents. And the LORD said unto Moses, *Make thee a fiery serpent, and set it upon a pole: and it shall come to pass, that everyone that is bitten, when he looketh upon it, shall live. And Moses made a serpent of brass, and put it upon a pole, and it came to pass, that if a serpent had bitten any man, when he beheld the serpent of brass, he lived* (Numbers 21:8-9). This was a symbolic representation of the crucifixion of Jesus Christ which was to happen several centuries later. I have seen an unusual painting on the crucifixion in which a serpent had been drawn, winding around the cross upon which the sacred body of our Lord was nailed, with the serpent's head nailed underneath the feet of Jesus signifying that the old serpent and death were spiritually crucified along with Jesus. The cross of Jesus has been lifted on Mount Calvary so that people, of all subsequent generations, can look upon it and can receive forgiveness of sins and wholesome health for the body, mind, and soul. In the 'Sacred Songs and Solos' compiled by Ira D. Sankey, we read and sing as follows:

> *Look, and thou shalt live*
> *Look, and thou shalt live*
> *Look to the cross where He died for thee*
> *Look, and thou shalt live*
> (Hymn No:429, Sacred Songs & Solos[7])

There is only one way for the sin-chocked world to attain salvation. There is only one hope for the hopeless. It is the cross of Jesus Christ, more precisely, Jesus Christ of Nazareth who was crucified some two thousand years ago on the mount of Golgotha (Mount Calvary).

In Genesis, we read that LORD GOD created man in His own image from the dust of the earth and breathed the breath of life into his nostrils (Genesis 2:7). In Psalm 8, we can find that God placed man a little lower than angels and crowned him with glory and honour (Psalm 8:5). But when the first man and woman transgressed and sinned against God due to the machination of the devil (who assumed the form of a serpent), they lost their glory and honour. Their faces and minds were darkened, the spirit of the LORD left them forever, and God's curse came upon them. They became alienated from God and were driven out of the Garden of Eden, the abode of peace, tranquillity and the presence of God. Later, consumed by jealousy and hatred, their son Cain killed his own brother Abel and thus shed innocent blood upon the earth.

---

[7] Sankey, I. Sacred Songs and Solos. London: Marshall, Morgan, and Scott, 1981.

Thereafter, the whole world became increasingly polluted with blood. The earth has witnessed innumerable murders, massacres, genocides, suicides, violence, crime, rapes, arsons, lootings, and wars which have claimed millions of human lives. St. John writes: *For all that is in the world, the lust of the flesh, and the lust of the eyes, and the pride of life, is not of the Father, but is of the world* (I John 2:16). Man, created in the very image of God and breathed with His own holy breath, has lost his divine and even human virtues and values and has become a brutal beast with no purpose in life. Romans 3:23 states: *For all have sinned, and come short of the glory of God.* In Romans 6:23, we read: *For the wages of sin is death; but the gift of God is eternal life through Jesus Christ our Lord.* It is a sad fact that although many profess to be Christians, they have not even obtained the first step in Christianity - the new birth. Further, although they fall victim to diverse temptations and sins, yet they claim to be perfect. But I John 1:8-9 clarifies: *If we say that we have no sin, we deceive ourselves, and the truth is not in us. If we confess our sins, he is faithful and just to forgive us our sins, and to cleanse us from all unrighteousness.*

Jesus related an example of those who despised others and trusted themselves to be righteous: *Two men went up into the temple to pray; the one a Pharisee, and the other a publican. The Pharisee stood and prayed thus with himself, God, I thank thee, that I am not as other men are, extortioners, unjust, adulterers, or even as this publican. I fast twice in the week, I give tithes of all that I possess. And the publican, standing afar off, would not lift up so much as his eyes unto heaven, but smote upon His breast, saying, God be merciful unto me a sinner* (Luke 18:10-13). The publican's prayer was heard by God, and he went home justified, whereas the Pharisee, who justified himself, went home unjustified before God.

Chapter 7 of St.Luke records a true incident that happened during the public ministry of Jesus Christ. Jesus was participating in a feast at the house of a Pharisee, when a sinful woman of the city, after knowing that he was there, came and stood weeping behind him. She fell down at his feet, and after washing them with her bitter tears, wiped them with the hairs of her head. She then kissed his feet, and anointed his feet with an alabaster box of ointment, which she broke there. Upon observing this, the Pharisee, who had invited Jesus, thought to himself, *This man, if he were a prophet, would have known who and what manner of woman this is that toucheth him: for she is a sinner.* Jesus, perceiving his thoughts, related a parable to him: *There was a certain creditor which had two debtors: the one owed five hundred pence, and the other fifty. And when they had nothing to pay, he frankly forgave them both.* Then, to the Pharisee, Jesus asked which of the two debtors would love the creditor most? The Pharisee replied that it would be the debtor whose greater debt was forgiven. Jesus admits that his reply was correct, but continues: *I entered into thine house, thou gavest me no water for my feet: but she hath washed my feet with tears, and wiped them with the hairs of her head. Thou gavest me no kiss; but this woman since the time I came in hath not ceased to kiss my feet. My head with oil thou didst not anoint: but this woman hath anointed my feet with ointment. Wherefore I say unto thee, Her sins, which are many, are forgiven; for she loved much: but to whom little is forgiven, the same loveth little* (Luke 7:44-47). Who was this self-righteous Pharisee who invited Jesus for the feast? None other than Simon the leper (Matthew 26:6-13)! In those days, lepers, forced to live outside the city in caves or abandoned houses, were not allowed to have domestic or social contacts, let alone conduct feasts! One might ask, "But, if so, how could Simon the leper hold the feast?" It was a thanksgiving, held because of his miraculous healing by the touch of Jesus our Lord. Yet, he never bothered to receive and honour Jesus in the traditional Jewish way. Moreover, when he saw Jesus' feet being washed by the sinful woman, he conveniently forgot that it was Jesus who healed him from leprosy and restored him back into his household and society. In fact, he even doubted whether Jesus was a prophet after all! What a pity! Moreover, he judged the woman although he himself was not at all righteous, for had he been righteous, he would have surely received Jesus with all his heart, mind, and soul.

This same incident is recorded in Chapter 26, verses 6 to 13, of the gospel according to St. Matthew, but with an additional category of accusers. They asked: *To what purpose is this waste? For this ointment might have been sold for much, and given to the poor. When Jesus understood it, he said unto them, Why trouble ye the woman? for she hath wrought a good work upon me. For ye have the poor always with you; but me ye have not always. For in that she hath poured this ointment on my body, she did it for my burial. Verily I say unto you, Whersoever this gospel shall be preached in the whole world, there shall also this, that this woman hath done, be told for a memorial of her.* Jesus appreciated her gratitude's extravagance.

Yet another instance of true repentance is seen in Luke 19:1-10. During his final journey to Jerusalem, Jesus was passing through the city of Jericho. A rich man, Zacchaeus, the chief among the publicans, having heard that Jesus was coming, ran ahead and climbed up a sycamore tree to see him clearly without himself being noticed by any one. But when Jesus came to the place, he stopped, looked up, and saw him and called Zacchaeus by name, saying, *Zacchaeus, make haste, and come down; for today I must abide at thy house* (Luke 19:5). He immediately came down and received him joyfully, and later vowed, *Behold, Lord, the half of my goods I give to the poor; and if I have taken anything from any man by false accusation, I restore him fourfold* (Luke 19:8). That is an accurate representation of the true repentance and new life.

I remember a man, in my city, who had such an experience when Jesus came into his heart. The very next day, he travelled all the way, to a far off city, to meet his elder brother, with whom he had a pending legal case, pertaining a property dispute. With a broken heart and conviction by the Holy Spirit, he embraced his brother and requested forgiveness, with tears trickling down from his eyes. His elder brother was also greatly moved and wept bitterly. They reconciled and were restored to true brotherhood. Soon, the court case was withdrawn and, even now, they live in harmony. On the other hand, we hear grievances from many, who accuse their own apparently pious Christian siblings of unlawfully robbing them of their possession. Is this not hypocrisy? Lord Jesus hates it utterly. We must reconcile with our siblings and neighbours and also with God, as stressed by Jesus in his Sermon on the Mount: *Therefore if thou bring thy gift to the altar, and there rememberest that thy brother hath aught against thee; Leave there thy gift before the altar, and go thy way; first be reconciled to thy brother, and then come and offer thy gift* (Matthew 5:23-24).

Dr. Radhakrishnan, the great philosopher and later President of India, remarked: "You Christians seem to us Hindus rather ordinary people making extraordinary claims."[8] Why did he make such an observation? Although we preach around about Christian values and virtues and encourage others to espouse such values and virtues, yet none of these are found in our practical lives! Thus, we are mostly professing Christians and not practising Christians. It is this attitude of ours which poses as a great stumbling block for many who are attracted to the Christian faith after reading or hearing the gospel message. We promise golden thrones in heaven, but hesitate to offer even a wooden chair to the new believer who comes to us. We speak of the great banquet in heaven, but hesitate to give even a glass of water to the thirsty stranger who requests for it. Jesus wants us to love even our enemies and to do good to those that hate us. It is not an insane request- after all, God loved us even when we were sinners and sent His only Son, Jesus Christ, to die for us, on the cross, in our place. Jesus asked: *For if ye love them which love you, what reward have ye? do not even the publicans the same? And if ye salute your brethren only, what do ye more than others? do not even the publicans so? Be ye therefore perfect, even as your Father which is in heaven is perfect* (Matthew 5: 46-48).

[8] Gopal, Sarvepalli. Radhakrishnan, a biography. Delhi: Oxford University Press, 1989.

Matthew was chosen when Jesus, at the very start of his ministry, came across him at the receipt of Customs. Upon hearing Jesus' words, *Follow me,* he immediately rose up and followed him, without even settling his account at the customs. He later arranged a feast, at his house, in honour of Jesus. When the Pharisees saw this, they asked Jesus disciples: *Why eateth your Master with publicans and sinners? But when Jesus heard that, he said unto them, They that be whole need not a physician, but they that are sick. But go ye and learn what that meaneth, I will have mercy, and not sacrifice: for I am not come to call the righteous, but sinners to repentance* (Matthew 9: 9-13).

In Chapter 15 of the gospel according to St. Luke, we read that when all the publicans and sinners drew near unto Jesus to hear him, the Pharisees and scribes murmured, *This man receiveth sinners, and eateth with them.* Then Jesus related three parables - the parable of the lost sheep, the lost coin, and the lost son. This wasn't a meaningless action- but one which illustrated his profound love for humans, even though they may wander away from him or even rebel against him. In the case of the lost sheep, when one sheep was missing from the flock of hundred sheep, the shepherd left the ninety-nine in the wilderness and went in search of the lost sheep, even after sunset. Upon finding it, he rejoiced, took it upon his shoulders, and brought into the sheep-hold. He even invited his friends and neighbours to partake in his happiness upon finding the lost sheep. Jesus explains: *I say unto you, that likewise joy shall be in heaven over one sinner that repenteth, more than over ninety and nine just persons, which need no repentance* (Luke 15:7).

There is a highly meaningful painting of Jesus depicted as the shepherd with the lost and found sheep upon his shoulders. The artist has vividly portrayed the wounds and thorn pricks on his sacred body, which he suffered whilst searching for the lost sheep. Jesus declares, in John 10: 11: *I am the good shepherd: the good shepherd giveth his life for the sheep.* Isaiah, in 53: 5-6, prophesies: *But he was wounded for our transgressions, he was bruised for our iniquities: the chastisement of our peace was upon him; and with his stripes we are healed. All we like sheep have gone astray; we have turned every one to his own way; and the LORD hath laid on him the iniquity of us all.*

In the parable of the lost silver coin, Jesus emphasises that each one of us are precious in the sight of God. When the woman realised that one of the silver coins was missing, she lit the lamp, diligently swept the room, found it, and rejoiced with her friends and neighbours. Jesus says: *Likewise, I say unto you, there is joy in the presence of the angels of God over one sinner that repenteth* (Luke 15:10).

We might be familiar with the parable of the lost son, more famously known as the parable of the prodigal son. The younger son rebelled against his loving Father, in spite of all the glories he had with him. He wanted to get his share of wealth and live independently in order to enjoy the pleasures of this world. We might have heard of similar incidents happening even in good Christian homes. The youngsters are keen to leave home and enjoy the vilest pleasures of the sinful world. This attitude had started even at the Garden of Eden when Adam and Eve sinned and wanted to avoid the presence of God. From thence till the present, man has been trying to run away from God. In his book "Runaway World"[9], Rev. Michael Green vividly described how people run away from God, run away from life's realities, run away from responsibilities, and run away from opportunities. What is the net result? The whole life is materially and spiritually ruined. In the parable, the rebellious son (with his opportunistic new friends) enjoys life, but wastes all his money. He eventually lands up working in a piggery since there was no other means to earn a livelihood. He even had to eat pigs' food to appease his hunger. It was in that miserable situation that he comes back to

---

[9] Green, Michael. Runaway World. Chicago: Inter-Varsity Press, 1968.

his senses. He thought: *How many hired servants of my father's have bread enough and to spare, and I perish with hunger! I will arise and go to my father, and will say unto him, Father, I have sinned against heaven, and before thee, And am no more worthy to be called thy son: make me as one of thy hired servants. And he arose, and came to his father. But when he was yet a great way off, his father saw him, and had compassion, and ran, and fell on his neck, and kissed him. And the son said unto him, Father, I have sinned against heaven, and in thy sight, and am no more worthy to be called thy son. But the father said to his servants, Bring forth the best robe, and put it on him: and put a ring on his hand, and shoes on his feet: And bring hither the fatted calf, and kill it: and let us eat, and be merry: For this my son was dead, and is alive again; he was lost, and is found. And they began to be merry* (Luke 15: 17-24). And if that is the love and forgiveness of an earthly father, then how much more will be that of our loving heavenly Father, as stated in Psalm 103 verses 8 to 13: *The LORD is merciful and gracious, slow to anger, and plenteous in mercy. He will not always chide: neither will he keep his anger for ever. He hath not dealt with us after our sins; nor rewarded us according to our iniquities. For as the heaven is high above the earth, so great is his mercy toward them that fear him. And as far as the east is from the west, so far hath he removed our transgressions from us. Like as a father pitieth his children, so the LORD pitieth them that fear him* (Psalm 103: 8 -13). We also read in Romans 5:8-11: *But God commendeth his love toward us, in that, while we were yet sinners, Christ died for us. Much more then, being now justified by his blood, we shall be saved from wrath through him. For if, when we were enemies, we were reconciled to God by the death of his Son, much more, being reconciled, we shall be saved by his life. And not only so, but we also joy in God through our Lord Jesus Christ, by whom we have now received the atonement.* Our loving God gave us the greatest possible gift – His one and only begotten and most beloved Son, Jesus Christ, to bear all our sins, iniquities, sorrows, and sicknesses, and to die on the most shameful cross, between two thieves, and to purchase all nations, tongues, and races of humanity, through his most precious blood so that we will be granted eternal redemption. God the Father loves us all; Jesus loves us all – including the worst sinner and even the brute who torments the Church. Jesus wants each and everyone to come to their senses, repent, and come to him; for all creatures are his own creations; and, all are his own children. I knew a mother who used to sit up, even late at night, awaiting her prodigal son who had become a notorious criminal and was hated by his own brothers and sisters. The mother used to serve him dinner every night, without being discovered by his own family members or by the police who were hunting for him. The Lord says in Isaiah 49:15: *Can a woman forget her sucking child, that she should not have compassion on the son of her womb? yea, they may forget, yet will I not forget thee.*

In Jeremiah 31:3 the LORD says: *I have loved thee with an everlasting love: therefore with loving kindness I have drawn thee.* This reminds me of a tense *drama in real life* which happened, four decades ago, in Munnar, a well-known hill station in Southern India, famous for tea plantations. A young Agricultural Officer, with his wife and little son, were residing in the plantation quarters. This young son was very hyperactive and loved to ramble around the house premises. One day, all of a sudden, the parents heard the distant screams of their son. When they rushed to the spot from where the screams originated, they saw that the boy had fallen into a narrow pit, several meters below the ground level. Although he was alive and sported minor injuries, he was so frightened that he screamed relentlessly. The neighbours too came running, but realised that rescue efforts were impossible- for the pit was so narrow that no one could descend on a rope and rescue him. On realising that no one would rescue the boy, his father took a long rope, tied his feet together, and requested: "Please lower me into the pit, in a head over heels position, so that I can pull him up. You can pull the rope out of the pit once I catch hold of him." Obviously, the bystanders were shocked by what seemed like stupidity. They repeatedly warned and tried to dissuade him, for it was certain he would die during the rescue operation. But he insisted and the people, hesitatingly, helped him. With his head and hands down, the father descended into the pity and caught hold of the boy. Those above ground pulled them to safety. Now as I write, the father is a grand old man and the boy is a well-employed man. Nobody else had ventured to take this risky job even though they were offered huge remuneration. Had they waited for the police and rescue team to arrive, the boy would have died due to anoxia and fear. It was nothing but the immediate, daring selfless action of the father which saved the boy's life. The father took a great risk only because of his relationship with the boy. If this be the love and concern of an earthly father, how much more would be the love and concern of our loving heavenly Father!

You may have read a tragic incident which happened in Rome several years ago. A little boy fell into a deep and narrow pit, so narrow that no one dared to go down. The police dug another pit parallel to it and tried to reach out for the boy's hands. Unfortunately, he slipped further down, because of the loose mud. The police continued their rescue efforts. The rescue workers dropped hot food and woollen clothing into the pit to keep the boy alive. Even the Italian President rushed to the scene to cheer up the boy. Alas! Those above ground were distressed to realise that the boy's voice was growing weaker. In fact, he eventually died due to hypothermia and anoxia. Everybody mourned the death of this sweet little boy. Even now, when I think of that incident, my eyes become wet.

God is love. He loves each and every one. He does not want anyone to perish materially or spiritually. But sin is a horrible pit. It does not have a steady ground where we can remain without slipping. No, in fact, it is worse than a miry clay or quick sand. The more one struggles and tries to escape from it, the more he slips down into the abyss. Psalm 40 begins with the following verses: *I waited patiently for the LORD; and he inclined unto me, and heard my cry. He brought me up also out of an horrible pit, out of the miry clay, and set my feet upon a rock, and established my goings. And he hath put a new song in my mouth, even praise unto our God: many shall see it, and fear, and shall trust in the LORD.*

Like the good shepherd searching for his lost sheep, Jesus came in search of you and me who, because of our own folly, had fallen into the abyss of sin and agony. Upon finding us in that perilous pit, he did not abandon us, unlike other passers-by who did not have any love and compassion to save us. Instead, Jesus came down into the abyss, all the while keeping himself spotless, and pulled us out of the stinking miry clay. He brought us out, washed us, cleansed us with his own precious blood, clothed us with the robe of his righteousness, gave us his ring of God's heirship, and gave us shoes for the preparation of the gospel of the kingdom of God. He gave us a new song in our mouths, even praise unto our gracious heavenly Father. Moreover, to redeem us from the bondage of the devil, Jesus paid the ultimate ransom by shedding his blood.

In Romans 8:31-32, it is written: *What shall we then say to these things? If God be for us, who can be against us? He that spared not his own Son, but delivered him up for us all, how shall he not with him also freely give us all things?* Shall I attempt at listing a fraction of what God has freely given us? Truly God gave us this beautiful planet to live and flourish in. He gave us sunshine, rains, and all natural resources. He established sun, moon, and stars so that we would know the time, seasons, and years, not to mention sources of light. He moulded us into bodies in His own likeness and made us fearfully and wonderfully. He bestowed us with intelligence and wisdom, along with all the means for our progress. He gave us good parents, good partners, good children, and good friends. He provided us with good jobs, good positions, and good possessions. He gave us His Holy Word, the Church, and His Holy Spirit. But the greatest of all gifts is His own only begotten Son JESUS, who was with Him even before the foundation of the world and heaven, who took human form in the historic person of Jesus Christ of Nazareth, two thousand years ago, and brought us eternal salvation through His sacrificial death on the cross.

> *To God be the glory! Great things He hath done!*
> *So loved He the world that He gave us His son;*
> *Who yielded His life an atonement for sin,*
> *And opened the Life-gate that all may go in*
> *Praise the Lord! Praise the Lord! Let the earth hear His voice!*
> *Praise the Lord! Praise the Lord! Let the people rejoice!*
> *Oh, come to the Father, through Jesus the Son;*
> *And give Him the glory-great things He hath done!*
> (Hymn No: 23, Sacred Songs and Solos[10])

Shall we join in prayer, giving thanks unto God for granting His only begotten Son Jesus Christ for us?

Our loving heavenly Father,

We praise thee, we adore thee, we worship thee, we magnify thee, we thank thee, and we bless thee for granting us thy only begotten Son Jesus Christ, who was in Thy bosom even before the foundation of the worlds, to come down into this sin sick earth to live as the son of man but without any sin and to lead a mode life of holiness and sacrifice to console the suffering, to heal the sick, to heal the broken hearted, to deliver the demon possessed, to raise the dead, to preach the gospel of the kingdom of God, to save millions of sinners through His teachings and kind deeds, and ultimately grant eternal salvation for all through His sufferings and agonising death on the cross. Our hearts overwhelm with repentance and gratitude. We thank Thee from the bottom of our hearts. We dedicate ourselves as living sacrifices and humble tributes before Thee. In Jesus' matchless name we pray, Amen.

---

[10] Sankey, I. Sacred Songs and Solos. London: Marshall, Morgan, and Scott, 1981.

4

JESUS CHRIST – THE LAMB OF GOD

THAT TAKES AWAY THE SIN OF THE WORLD

The next day John seeth Jesus coming unto him, and saith, Behold the Lamb of God, which taketh away the sin of the world

John 1:29

John the Baptist was appointed by God to prepare the path for Jesus Christ, as foretold by prophet Isaiah: *The voice of him that crieth in the wilderness, Prepare ye the way of the LORD, make straight in the desert a highway for our God* (Isaiah 40:3). The Jews had been eagerly waiting for the appearance of Messiah, or Christ, for their physical deliverance from Roman bondage. When John the Baptist began his ministry by the banks of the river Jordan, preaching about repentance and baptising those who repented of their sins, the Jews sent priests and Levites from Jerusalem to enquire whether he was the much-anticipated Christ. John replied: *I am not the Christ... I am the voice of one crying in the wilderness, Make straight the way of the LORD, as said the prophet Esaias* (John 1:20, 23). When they asked him why then was he baptising the people, he answered, *I baptize with water: but there standeth one among you, whom ye know not: He it is, who coming after me is preferred before me, whose shoe's latchet I am not worthy to unloose* (John 1:26-27). In Matthew 3:11-12 we read John the Baptist's words as follows: *I indeed baptize you with water unto repentance: but he that cometh after me is mightier than I, whose shoes I am not worthy to bear: he shall baptize you with the Holy Ghost, and with fire: Whose fan is in his hand, and he will thoroughly purge his floor, and gather his wheat into the garner; but he will burn up the chaff with unquenchable fire.* John 1:29-35 continues with what happened: *The next*

44

day John seeth Jesus coming unto him, and saith, Behold the Lamb of God, which taketh away the sin of the world. This is he of whom I said, After me cometh a man which is preferred before me: for he was before me. And I knew him not: but that he should be made manifest to Israel, therefore am I come baptizing with water. And John bare record, saying, "I saw the Spirit descending from heaven like a dove, and it abode upon him. And I knew him not: but he that sent me to baptize with water, the same said unto me, Upon whom thou shalt see the Spirit descending, and remaining on him, the same is he which baptizeth with the Holy Ghost. And I saw, and bare record that this is the Son of God. Again the next day after John stood, and two of his disciples; And looking upon Jesus as he walked, he saith, Behold the Lamb of God! Upon hearing this, the two disciples left John and followed Jesus.

Throughout the Old Testament are instances in which a lamb or ram or a bullock is sacrificed, either as a propitiation for sins of the people or as a thanks offering unto the Lord. In Genesis 3:21 we read as follows: *Unto Adam also and to his wife did the LORD God make coats of skins, and clothed them.* This implies that, to cover the nakedness of Adam and Eve, God killed some animals and used their skins to clothe them. Thus, God Himself made the first animal sacrifice to save the first man and woman from shame. The second incident was when Cain and Abel brought offerings unto the Lord (in Genesis 4:4). Abel sacrificed the firstlings from his flock and God was pleased with him and his sacrifice. Then, after several years, as a thanksgiving for having saved him and his family from the great flood which destroyed all the dwellers of the world, Noah built an altar, took one from each clean beasts and clean fowls, and made a burnt offering unto Lord. Later, Abram (before God changed his name to Abraham) sacrificed a heifer, a she-goat, and a ram (all three-year olds), as well as a turtledove and a young pigeon (Genesis 15:9-10).

The sacrifice of a lamb or a ram as a perfect substitute for human sacrifice is implied in the great event recorded in Genesis. In order to test the faith of Abraham, God commanded him: *Take now thy son, thine only son Isaac, whom thou lovest, and get thee into the land of Moriah; and offer him there for a burnt offering upon one of the mountains which I will tell thee of* (Genesis 22:2). Without the least hesitation and with implicit obedience to God, Abraham took with him his only son, Isaac, and set off early in the morning. On the third day, he saw the place afar off and told his men to: *Abide ye here with the ass; and I and the lad will go yonder and worship, and come back again to you* (Genesis 22:5). Look at Abraham's faith: He was confident that he and his son would come back after the sacrifice. In the epistle to Hebrews, we read as follows: *By faith Abraham, when he was tried, offered up Isaac: and he that had received the promises offered up his only begotten son, Of whom it was said, That in Isaac shall thy seed be called: Accounting that God was able to raise him up, even from the dead; from whence also he received him in a figure* (Hebrews 11:17-19). In Genesis 22:6-8, the narration continues: *And Abraham took the wood of the burnt offering, and laid it upon Isaac his son; and he took the fire in his hand, and a knife; and they went both of them together. And Isaac spake unto Abraham his father, and said, My father, and he said, Here am I, my son. And he said, Behold the fire and the wood: but where is the lamb for a burnt offering? And Abraham said, My son, God will provide himself a lamb for a burnt offering: so they went both of them together.* We can attempt to guess the tension faced by Abraham and how much Isaac's words would have pierced through his loving heart! But he remained determined to obey God's commandment and sacrifice his only son born in his grand old age. Yet he believed that God would provide Himself a lamb for a burnt offering. *And they came to the place which God had told him of; and Abraham built an altar there, and laid the wood in order, and bound Isaac his son, and laid him on the altar upon the wood. And Abraham stretched forth his hand, and took the knife to slay his son. And the angel of the LORD called unto him out of heaven, and said, Abraham, Abraham: and he said, Here am I. And he said, Lay not thine hand upon the lad, neither do thou any thing unto him: for now I know that thou fearest God, seeing thou hast not withheld thy son, thine only son from me. And Abraham lifted up his eyes, and looked, and behold behind him a ram caught in a thicket by his horns: and Abraham went and took the ram, and offered him up for a burnt offering in the stead of his son* (Genesis 22:9-13). The most important point, which I want to emphasise, is that God provided Abraham with a ram, in that desolate mountain, for a burnt offering, instead of Isaac. Thus, in the place where a youth had to die, God sent a ram instead. This ram is the symbolic representation of Jesus Christ, the Lamb of God who takes away the sin of the world. The second point to be emphasised is the absolute obedience of Isaac towards his father, so lovingly referred to earlier as 'My father'. How much would he have been surprised and startled when his father bound him, all of a sudden, and placed him upon the logs on the altar, and took out his knife to sacrifice him! Perhaps, he would have even thought that his father became mad. Yet, without a word or a scream, he waited for his death at the hands of his own most beloved father. This is, in fact, a reflection of the absolute obedience of Jesus Christ to the will of the Father to sacrifice Jesus on the shameful cross. In Isaiah 53:7, we read thus: *He was oppressed, and he was afflicted, yet he opened not his mouth: he is brought as a lamb to the slaughter, and as a sheep before her shearers is dumb, so he openeth not his mouth.* Also in Philippians 2:5-8, we can find: *Let this mind be in you, which was also in Christ Jesus: Who, being in the form of God, thought it not robbery to be equal with God, But made himself of no reputation, and took upon him the form of a servant, and was made in the likeness of men: And being found in fashion as a man, he humbled himself, and became obedient unto death, even the death of the cross.* Perhaps, God would have wanted to convey to Abraham that animal sacrifices would have to be continued for the remission of sins until He would sacrifice, at the appropriate time, His only begotten son Jesus Christ for the redemption of the entire mankind once and for all.

The institution of Passover, as commanded by God to Moses in the land of Egypt before the deliverance of the Israelites, is another great event which proclaims the importance of the unblemished lamb and its blood to escape from the death of human beings. Let me quote from the Bible: God spoke to Moses and Aaron: *Speak ye unto all the congregation of Israel, saying, In the tenth day of this month they shall take to them every man a lamb, according to the house of their fathers, a lamb for an house: And if the household be too little for the lamb, let him and his neighbour next unto his house take it according to the number of the souls; every man according to his eating shall make your count for the lamb. Your lamb shall be without blemish, a male of the first year: ye shall take it out from the sheep, or from the goats: And ye shall keep it up until the fourteenth day of the same month: and the whole assembly of the congregation of Israel shall kill it in the evening. And they shall take of the blood, and strike it on the two side posts and on the upper door post of the houses, wherein they shall eat it. And they shall eat the flesh in that night, roast with fire, and unleavened bread; and with bitter herbs they shall eat it ..., And thus shall ye eat it; with your loins girded, your shoes on your feet, and your staff in your hand; and ye shall eat it in haste: it is the LORD'S passover. For I will pass through the land of Egypt this night, and I will smite all the firstborn in the land of Egypt, both man and beast; and against all the gods of Egypt I will execute judgment: I am the LORD. And the blood shall be to you for a token upon the houses where ye are: and when I see the blood, I will pass over you, and the plague shall not be upon you to destroy you, when I smite the land of Egypt. And this day shall be unto you for a memorial; and ye shall keep it a feast by an ordinance for ever* (Exodus 12:3-14). According to Lord's commandments, the Israelites observed the Passover with all seriousness and solemnity, and their firstborn children were spared the very night when all the firstborn of the Egyptians died instantaneously, including Pharaoh's eldest son, which forced him to send the Israelites out of Egypt that night itself.

During the Israelites' long journey from Egypt to the promised land of Canaan, Lord God summoned Moses to go up the mount of Sinai, where Moses spent forty days and forty nights in the presence of God. During this time, God not only gave Moses the two tablets of stone inscribed with the ten commandments written by His own finger, but He also explained to Moses about the ten commandments and other ordinances which the Israelites have to obey forever. After leaving the two tablets of stone before God, Moses came down and wrote God's words in a book. He built an altar and offered burnt offerings and sacrificial peace offerings of oxen unto the Lord. He read out to the Israelites the book of the covenant. And they said: *All the words which the LORD hath said will we do, and be obedient. And Moses took the blood, and sprinkled it on the people, and said, Behold the blood of the covenant, which the LORD hath made with you concerning all these words* (Exodus 24: 3, 7-8). Thus, the Old Testament (Old Covenant) was established between God and the children of Israel through the blood of the sacrificial animal. The New Testament, however, was established by Jesus Christ, through the institution of Lord's Supper, through his own flesh and blood.

Afterwards, Moses built the tabernacle as a mobile abode for the Lord. Throughout their journey thenceforth, the Ark of the Covenant, containing the Ten Commandments and all other materials, was carried by the Israelites wherever they went. God's mighty presence manifested in the form of a cloudy pillar during daytime and in the form of a pillar of fire by night. Whenever the cloudy pillar moved, the Israelites dismantled the tabernacle and their tents and followed its path. When it stopped, they too stopped and pitched their tents and installed the tabernacle.

The instructions given by God on constructing the tabernacle is written in Exodus Chapters 26 and 27. The plan of the mobile tabernacle may be abstracted as follows: The tabernacle was a large and splendid tent with a large single entrance leading to a large area for the congregation to assemble. Curtains separated this assembly area from the holy place, which only the priests could access and which featured altars for performing sacrifices. Still further on, separated by a single, long veil/curtain, was the most holy place (the Holy of Holies) where the Ark of the Covenant, made of cedar wood, was placed.

The Ark contained the two tablets with the inscription of the Ten Commandments written for the second time by God (for the first set of tablets was broken by Moses whilst angry at the Israelites who worshipped a molten golden calf). A golden vessel containing manna and the sprouted rod of Aaron were also placed inside it. Above the ark was positioned the golden Mercy Seat, with the figurines of two cherubs facing each other. God's glory was always there upon the mercy seat.

Only the high priest could access this most holy place, and that too only once a year, precisely on the Day of Atonement, after having cleansed his own sins and sins of the congregation with the blood of the sacrificial animals and with the burning of incense. Leviticus chapter 16 enumerates the procedures to be followed by the high priest on the Day of Atonement:

Early in the morning, he washes his body with water and puts on holy garments. He takes two unblemished goat kids at the entrance of the tabernacle and casts lots on these to decide which should be used for sin offering and which to be sent out as the scapegoat. Then, he takes a bullock into the holy place of the tabernacle, cuts its throat, and collects its blood in a golden vessel. Next, in a censor, he takes coals of fire from the altar and sprinkles incense upon it so that its sweet perfume spreads and permeates into the holy place and into most holy place. After that, he carries the collected blood of the bullock and the censor with the cloudy smoke of incense into the most holy place so that the vapours of the incense cover the Mercy Seat upon the Ark of the Covenant. He sprinkles the bullock's blood, seven times with his finger, upon the Mercy Seat. Without the blood of the bullock and the cloud of incense, even the high priest could not go into the presence of the Lord. This is for the sin offering and atonement of himself and his family.

Then, walking backwards, he emerges out from the most holy place. He picks up the goat kid for sin offering, kills it at the holy place of the tabernacle, and collects its blood in another golden vessel. Again, he enters the most holy place, carrying along with him the censor containing the cloudy smoke of incense, and sprinkles the kid's blood upon the Mercy Seat seven times as before. Then he walks backward into the holy place and makes atonement at the altar. For the atonement of the congregation, he comes out into the tabernacle of congregation and sanctifies it by sprinkling the blood of the bullock and the goat's kid. During this ceremony, the people are not permitted to enter into the tabernacle.

The high priest then lays both his hands upon the head of the scapegoat, and confesses and confers upon it all the iniquities of the people. The scapegoat is then driven out into the wilderness. After this, he changes his attire, washes himself with water, and puts on his priestly robes. He takes an unblemished ram into the holy place, sacrifices it upon the altar, and performs the burnt offering, thereby making the atonement for himself and for the congregation. The word 'atonement' means making amends for a wrong or injury.

Although these acts may appear strange to the non-Jew, every act performed on the Day of Atonement has profound spiritual meaning. These were, in fact, symbolic events which foretold the total atonement brought about by Jesus Christ, the Lamb of God, several centuries later. Both the authoritative Webster's New World Dictionary[11] and Oxford English Dictionary[12] explain atonement as 'the reconciliation of God and mankind through Jesus Christ' (ed: merged definition). Indeed, Jesus Christ assumed the role of the scapegoat when he walked, all the way from the Roman governor's palace to Golgotha, bearing the cursed cross upon his shoulder and a

---

[11] Guralnik, D. eds. Webster's New World Dictionary. 2nd ed. New Delhi: Oxford and IBH Publishing Company, 1975.
[12] http://oxforddictionaries.com/definition/english/atonement?q=atonement

crown of thorns upon his sacred head, amidst the incessant cruel mockery and scourging, all the time bearing the sins and iniquities of the entire humanity. Thus, he suffered shame and went out of the city into 'the place of skulls' (Golgotha), where criminals were crucified by the Roman government.

Secondly, he played the role of the sacrificial bullock and goat's kid when he offered himself on the cursed cross and shed even the last drop of his blood for the atonement of sins. He willingly received the punishment due for sinners on his entire body, mind, and soul.

Thirdly, he became the High Priest, by entering into the presence of God, not with the blood of sacrificial animals, but with his own blood, and achieved eternal salvation for the mankind. In the epistle to Hebrews Chapter 9, verses 11 and 12, St. Paul writes: *But Christ being come an high priest of good things to come, by a greater and more perfect tabernacle, not made with hands, that is to say, not of this building; Neither by the blood of goats and calves, but by his own blood he entered in once into the holy place, having obtained eternal redemption for us.* St.Paul continues: *For when Moses had spoken every precept to all the people according to the law, he took the blood of calves and of goats, with water, and scarlet wool, and hyssop, and sprinkled both the book, and all the people, Saying, This is the blood of the testament which God hath enjoined unto you. Moreover he sprinkled with blood both the tabernacle, and all the vessels of the ministry. And almost all things are by the law purged with blood; and without shedding of blood is no remission. It was therefore necessary that the patterns of things in the heavens should be purified with these; but the heavenly things themselves with better sacrifices than these. For Christ is not entered into the holy places made with hands, which are the figures of the true; but into heaven itself, now to appear in the presence of God for us: Nor yet that he should offer himself often, as the high priest entereth into the holy place every year with the blood of others; For then must he often have suffered since the foundation of the world: but now once in the end of the world hath he appeared to put away sin by the sacrifice of himself. And as it is appointed unto men once to die, but after this the judgment: So Christ was once offered to bear the sins of many; and unto them that look for him shall he appear the second time without sin unto salvation* (Hebrews 9:19-28).

Further, in the book of Isaiah Chapter 53, verses 3 to 5, it is written: *He is despised and rejected of men; a man of sorrows, and acquainted with grief: and we hid as it were our faces from him; he was despised, and we esteemed him not. Surely he hath borne our griefs, and carried our sorrows: yet we did esteem him stricken, smitten of God, and afflicted. But he was wounded for our transgressions, he was bruised for our iniquities: the chastisement of our peace was upon him; and with his stripes we are healed.* St.Peter writes: *Forasmuch as ye know that ye were not redeemed with corruptible things, as silver and gold, from your vain conversation received by tradition from your fathers; But with the precious blood of Christ, as of a lamb without blemish and without spot: Who verily was foreordained before the foundation of the world, but was manifest in these last times for you* (I Peter 1:18-20).

The institution of the Lord's supper, in the place of the traditional Jewish Passover, further explains the true meaning of the Passover ceremony. The gospels write thus: *And as they did eat, Jesus took bread, and blessed, and brake it, and gave to them, and said, Take, eat: this is my body. And he took the cup, and when he had given thanks, he gave it to them: and they all drank of it. And he said unto them, This is my blood of the new testament, which is shed for many. Verily I say unto you, I will drink no more of the fruit of the vine, until that day that I drink it new in the kingdom of God* (Mark 14: 22-25). Obviously, this was a symbolic event of giving his own body and blood to the disciples for their atonement and salvation. But this was not only for them alone, but for all those who believe in this sacrament and receive it with all humility, obedience, and piety. Jesus had already told his disciples and others around him: *Verily, verily, I say unto you, Except ye eat the flesh of the Son of man, and drink his blood, ye have no life in you. Whoso eateth my flesh, and drinketh my blood, hath eternal life; and I will raise him up at the last day. For my flesh is meat indeed, and my blood is drink indeed* (John 6:53-55). Only on the next day did the disciples understand the significance of the Lord's supper, upon seeing the thoroughly bruised, wounded, and battered sacred body of Jesus Christ, whose holy blood was shed even upto the very last drop. When Jesus finally gave up his soul into the hands of his heavenly Father, the veil of the temple of Jerusalem was rent in twain, from the top to the bottom, exposing the most holy place, which was hitherto inaccessible to the people. Thus, his sacrifice demolished the wall of separation between the most holy God and sinful men, as explained by St Paul in the 9th chapter of Hebrews. Hence, we have access to the throne of grace, solely through the blood of Jesus Christ, the Lamb of God.

The importance of the shedding of blood can be understood from God's own statements recorded in Leviticus 17:11-14: *For the life of the flesh is in the blood: and I have given it to you upon the altar to make an atonement for your souls: for it is the blood that maketh an atonement for the soul. Therefore I said unto the children of Israel, No soul of you shall eat blood, neither shall any stranger that sojourneth among you eat blood. And whatsoever man there be of the children of Israel, or of the strangers that sojourn among you, which hunteth and catcheth any beast or fowl that may be eaten; he shall even pour out the blood thereof, and cover it with dust. For it is the life of all flesh; the blood of it is for the life thereof: therefore I said unto the children of Israel, Ye shall eat the blood of no manner of flesh: for the life of all flesh is the blood thereof: whosoever eateth it shall be cut off.* It is written in Hebrews 9:22: *And almost all things are by the law purged with blood; and without shedding of blood is no remission.* In addition to the shedding the blood of sacrificial animals on the Day of Atonement, similar sacrifices were performed throughout the year as sin offerings of individuals in the congregation. This demonstrates that a lamb, or a goatling, or a ram, or a bullock had to die for the remission of sins instead of the real sinner. Jesus Christ took the role of all these sacrificial animals, in addition to that of the Passover lamb, and achieved eternal salvation of the people of all millennia, both Jews and Gentiles. St John writes in the book of Revelation: *And I beheld, and, lo, in the midst of the throne and of the four beasts, and in the midst of the elders, stood a Lamb as it had been slain, having seven horns and seven eyes, which are the seven Spirits of God sent forth into all the earth. And he came and took the book out of the right hand of him that sat upon the throne. And when he had taken the book, the four beasts and four and twenty elders fell down before the Lamb, having every one of them harps, and golden vials full of odours, which are the prayers of saints. And they sung a new song, saying, Thou art worthy to take the book, and to open the seals thereof; for thou wast slain, and hast redeemed us to God by thy blood out of every kindred, and tongue, and people, and nation; And hast made us unto our God kings and priests: and we shall reign on the earth. And I beheld, and I heard the voice of many angels round about the throne and the beasts and the elders: and the number of them was ten thousand times ten thousand, and thousands of thousands; Saying with a loud voice, Worthy is the Lamb that was slain to receive power, and riches, and wisdom, and strength, and honour, and glory, and blessing. And every creature which is in heaven, and on the earth, and under the earth, and such as are in the sea, and all that are in them, heard I saying, Blessing, and honour, and glory, and power, be unto him that sitteth upon the throne, and unto the Lamb for ever and ever. And the four beasts said, Amen. And the four and twenty elders fell down and worshipped him that liveth for ever and ever* (Revelations 5:6-14).

Later on in Revelations, we read about the appearance of countless number of saints of God, chosen from all nations, who sing praises unto God and the Lamb (Jesus Christ): *After this I beheld, and, lo, a great multitude, which no man could number, of all nations, and kindreds, and people, and tongues, stood before the throne, and before the Lamb, clothed with white robes, and with palms in their hands; And cried with a loud voice saying, Salvation to our God which sitteth upon the throne, and unto the Lamb. And all the angels stood round about the throne, and about the elders and the four beasts, and fell before the throne on their faces, and worshipped God, Saying, Amen: Blessing, and glory, and wisdom, and thanksgiving, and honour, and power, and might, be unto our God for ever and ever. Amen. And one of the elders answered, saying unto me, What are these which are arrayed in white robes? and whence came they? And I said unto him, Sir, thou knowest. And he said to me, These are they which came out of great tribulation, and have washed their robes, and made them white in the blood of the Lamb. Therefore are they before the throne of God, and serve him day and night in his temple: and he that sitteth on the throne shall dwell among them* (Revelations 7:9-15). This is the blessed privilege given to the elect of God, bestowed upon them children only through the blood of Jesus. As St.John writes: *This then is the message which we have heard of him, and declare unto you, that God is light, and in him is no darkness at all. If we say that we have fellowship with him, and walk in darkness, we lie, and do not the truth: But if we walk in the light, as he is in the light, we have fellowship one with another, and the blood of Jesus Christ his Son cleanseth us from all sin* (I John 1:5-7).

> *Would you be free from your burden of sin?*
> *There's power in the blood, power in the blood;*
> *Would you o'er evil a victory win?*
> *There's wonderful power in the blood.*
> *There is power, ... power, wonder working power*
> *In the blood.... of the Lamb;*
> *There is power, ... power, wonder-working power*
> *In the precious blood of the Lamb.*
> (Hymn No: 145, Sacred Songs and Solos[13])

> *Just as I am - without one plea,*
> *But that Thy blood was shed for me,*
> *And that Thou bidd'st me come to Thee,*
> *O Lamb of God, I come!*

> *Just as I am-poor, wretched, blind,*
> *Sight, riches, healing of the mind;*
> *Yea, all I need, in Thee to find,*
> *O Lamb of God, I come!*

> *Just as I am - Thou wilt receive,*
> *Wilt welcome, pardon, cleanse, relieve:*
> *Because thy promise I believe,*

---

[13] Sankey, I. Sacred Songs and Solos. London: Marshall, Morgan, and Scott, 1981.

O Lamb of God, I come!
(Hymn No: 473, Sacred Songs and Solos)

Now shall we have a word of prayer?

Our loving Lord and Saviour Jesus Christ, the Lamb of God that takes away the sins of the world, Have mercy on us. We repent with bitter tears for all the sins and transgressions we have committed against thee. We regret for causing so much sorrow for thee and so much sufferings for thee. Thou hast voluntarily suffered all these tortures, mockery, humiliation, and crucifixion simply because of bearing our sins in our place. Now Lord, forgive all our sins because of thy boundless love and grace. Wash us with thy precious blood; cleanse us with thy precious blood; grant us peace, joy and salvation. Fill us Lord with thy Holy Spirit and power. Protect us within thy precious blood. Use us for thy glory. In thy most precious name we pray Jesus, Amen.

5
JESUS CHRIST-THE LORD WHO HEALS

The Spirit of the Lord is upon me, because he hath anointed me to preach the gospel to the poor; he hath sent me to heal the broken hearted, to preach deliverance to the captives, and recovering of sight to the blind, to set at liberty them that are bruised, To preach the acceptable year of the Lord

Luke 4:18- 19

Lord Jesus Christ read out the above passage from the book of Isaiah when he went to the synagogue in his native town of Nazareth on a Sabbath day at the beginning of his ministry. He continued: *This day is this scripture fulfilled in your ears* (Luke 4:21).

Truly Jesus came down to earth to preach the gospel to the poor and to the meek; to heal the broken hearted, to preach deliverance to the captives, to recover the sight to the blind, to liberate them who were bruised and crushed, and to preach the acceptable year of the Lord, in the fullness of grace and power of the Holy Spirit, as prophesied in Isaiah 61:1-3. In fact, his sermon on the mount begins with the Beatitudes: *Blessed are the poor in spirit: for their's is the kingdom of heaven. Blessed are they that mourn: for they shall be comforted. Blessed are the meek: for they shall inherit the earth. Blessed are they which do hunger and thirst after righteousness: for they shall be filled...* (Matthew 5:3-6). His words over brimmed with grace, love, and compassion which were gratefully received by the thirsty multitudes longing for comfort and consolation. Once he cried out: *Come unto me, all ye that labour and are heavy laden, and I will give you rest* (Matthew 11:28).

God's chosen people, the Israelites, were under Roman rule during the time of Jesus' public ministry. They were heavily taxed and oppressed by the Romans. The Temple of Jerusalem could not offer them consolation since it was full of priests, Levites, and Pharisees who were eager to exploit them. All sicknesses were considered punishments imposed by God for the people's sins and transgressions. The priests and Pharisees imposed upon them heavy burdens of penalties in the forms of offerings and sacrifices which did not bestow any peace of mind. In fact, it was impossible to pray peacefully at the Temple because of the noisy businesses being conducted there, even inside the building itself! None was available to hear their grievances or to help them in any way. Given this background, it is hardly amazing that the words of Jesus presented a soothening balm to the burning hearts of thousands of people who followed him wherever he went. His words were filled with supernatural power and authority, causing them to be amazed and voice out, *What thing is this? what new doctrine is this? for with authority commandeth he even the unclean spirits, and they do obey him* (Mark 1:27).

Matthew 4:23-25 records as follows: *And Jesus went about all Galilee, teaching in their synagogues, and preaching the gospel of the kingdom, and healing all manner of sickness and all manner of disease among the people. And his fame went throughout all Syria: and they brought unto him all sick people that were taken with diverse diseases and torments, and those which were possessed with devils, and those which were lunatic, and those that had the palsy; and he healed them. And there followed him great multitudes of people from Galilee, and from Decapolis, and from Jerusalem, and from Judæa, and from beyond Jordan.* Also we read: *When the even was come, they brought unto him many that were possessed with devils: and he cast out the spirits with his word, and healed all that were* sick: *That it might be fulfilled which was spoken by Esaias the prophet, saying, Himself took our infirmities, and bare our sicknesses* (Matthew 8:16-17). In fact, ultimately healing comes from the sacred wounds of Jesus. In Matthew 9:35-36 we read: *And Jesus went about all the cities and villages, teaching in their synagogues, and preaching the gospel of the kingdom, and healing every sickness and every disease among the people. But when he saw the multitudes, he was moved with compassion on them, because they fainted, and were scattered abroad, as sheep having no shepherd.* Just like a loving mother who cannot forsake her afflicted child, Jesus, the creator of every human being, had unlimited love and compassion on the sick and the suffering. He touched them and healed them instantaneously.

Once a leper knelt before Jesus saying: *If thou wilt, thou canst make me clean* (Mark 1:40). In those days, lepers were greatly discriminated against and were shunned by the Jews. Whenever symptoms of leprosy were noticed in a person, irrespective of his social status and wealth, he was excommunicated from home and society. They were considered to be cursed; upon seeing one, the healthy Jews would hide their faces and flee. Lepers lived in isolation, far away from the civilisation, living on the mercy of some, and were prohibited from coming out in the public places. If they saw anyone, they were expected to identify themselves by shouting 'Unclean' and evade away. But this leper was bold enough to approach Jesus and kneel down before him, firmly believing that he will not drive him away, but will heal him, if he so wished. *And Jesus, moved with compassion, put forth his hand and touched him, and saith unto him, I will; be thou clean. And as soon as he had spoken, immediately the leprosy departed from him, and he was cleansed* (Mark 1:41-42). It is quite interesting to note that this incident happened just at the start of Jesus' public ministry.

At Capernaum, Jesus was preaching in a very packed house. Upon failing to approach Jesus through the thick crowd around him, the friends of a man sick of palsy broke open the roof of the house where he was at, and lowered the man in a bed. When Jesus saw their faith, he said unto the sick man, *Son, thy sins be forgiven thee* (Mark 2:5). The scribes, who were present there, reasoned to themselves that Jesus was saying blasphemy as only God could forgive sins. After immediately perceiving this, Jesus asked them, *Why reason ye these things in your hearts? Whether is it easier to say to the sick of the palsy, Thy sins be forgiven thee; or to say, Arise, and take up thy bed, and walk? But that ye may know that Son of man hath power on earth to forgive sins, (he saith to the sick of the palsy,) I say unto thee, Arise, and take up thy bed, and go thy way into thine house. And immediately he arose, took up the bed, and went before them all; insomuch that they were all amazed, and glorified God, saying, We never saw it on this fashion* (Mark 2:8-12). In this incident, Jesus first forgave the sins of the man with palsy, and then healed him. Since Jesus first said to the sick man that his sins have been forgiven, it is undeniable that sin would have been the root cause of this man's sickness.

This becomes clearer in the case of the helpless man who waited beside the pool of Bethesda for thirty-eight years, as recorded in Chapter 5 of the gospel according to St. John. *When Jesus saw him lie, and knew that he had been now a long time in that case, he saith unto him, Wilt thou be made whole? The impotent man answered him, Sir, I have no man, when the water is troubled, to put me into the pool: but while I am coming, another steppeth down before me. Jesus saith unto him, Rise, take up thy bed, and walk. And immediately the man was made whole, and took up his bed, and walked: and on the same day was the sabbath... Afterward Jesus findeth him in the temple, and said unto him, Behold, thou art made whole: sin no more, lest a worse thing come unto thee* (John 5:6-9; 14). It is very evident that this man's sinful life resulted in him becoming grievously sick for thirty-eight years, and Jesus cautions him not to sin any more lest a worse thing may happen. Yes, Jesus forgives his sins and heals him, but there is also a commandment not to sin again as is seen again in the case of the woman who was caught in adultery and brought before him, to whom he said, *Go, and sin no more* (John 8:11).

Some have a wrong notion that Jesus is always willing to forgive an individual's sins, even if he sins over and over again. Although Jesus knows human weaknesses, he has set himself as an example, before the whole humanity, of how one can follow his footprints, and live a spotless and saintly life. He forgives a truly repenting sinner, and sometimes, out of his boundless grace (as seen in the case of the man with palsy and the man at the Pool of Bethesda), this forgiveness is bestowed without the individual asking him. However, I believe that there is a limit for the forgiveness and long-suffering of Jesus and the heavenly Father. In Hebrews 10:26-31 thus it is written: *For if we sin wilfully after that we have received the knowledge of truth, there remaineth no more sacrifice for sins. But a certain fearful looking for of judgement and fiery indignation, which shall devour the adversaries. He that despised Moses' law died without mercy under two or three witnesses: Of how much sorer punishment, suppose ye, shall he be thought worthy, who hath trodden under foot the Son of God, and hath counted the blood of the covenant, wherewith he was sanctified, an unholy thing, and hath done despite unto the Spirit of grace? For we know him that hath said, Vengeance belongeth unto me, I will recompense, saith the Lord. And again, The Lord shall judge his people. It is a fearful thing to fall into the hands of the living God.* In I Corinthians 3:16-17, it is written: *Know ye not that ye are the temple of God, and that the Spirit of God dwelleth in you? If any man defile the temple of God, him shall God destroy; for the temple of God is holy, which temple ye are.*

Several sicknesses are caused by fornications. The incidence of sexually transmitted diseases is steadily increasing and the worst-case scenario even projects that HIV may wipe out the human race from the face of the earth, within a few decades, unless immediate preventive measures are taken. Several diseases are caused by unhealthy lifestyle choices. Tobacco habits are responsible for a major proportion of human ailments including cancer. Alcohol and narcotic drugs are also causing several serious diseases. Negligence is also a cause of various ailments. After all, "*Sound mind in a sound body*" is the age-old proverb. We may say: "*Sound soul in a sound body*". The gospel according to St. Luke describes the childhood of Jesus as follows: *And the child grew, and waxed strong in spirit, filled with wisdom: and the grace of God was upon him* (Luke 2:40). Joseph and Daniel in the Bible are also apt examples for everyone to emulate. But the best person to model ourselves upon is Jesus Christ himself. May our children and youth grow like him.

There are also sicknesses brought about by evil spirits, which may often baffle even the best doctors. It is only when these evil spirits are cast out by prayer that the afflicted recover to normalcy. All four Gospels provide accounts of Jesus casting out such demons. Perhaps the unique case is that of the man, at the shore of Gadarenes, possessed with a legion of demons: *who had his dwelling among the tombs; and no man could bind him, no, not with chains: Because that he had been often bound with fetters and chains, and the chains had been plucked asunder by him, and the fetters broken in pieces: neither could any man tame him. And always, night and day, he was in the mountains, and in the tombs, crying, and cutting himself with stones. But when he saw Jesus afar off, he ran and worshipped him, And cried with a loud voice, and said, What have I to do with thee, Jesus, thou Son of the most high God? I adjure thee by God, that thou torment me not. For he said unto him, Come out of the man, thou unclean spirit. And he asked him, What is thy name? And he answered, saying, My name is Legion: for we are many* (Mark 5:3-9). In the Roman army, a legion referred to a unit of thousands of soldiers. Therefore, this man was possessed by thousands of demons. If a single demon is capable of causing misery and havoc in the life of an individual, just imagine the pathetic plight of a man possessed with a legion of demons! But he came kneeling down before Jesus Christ, the King of Kings and Lord of Lords, before whom all demons tremble and flee. When Jesus cast out the demons and set the man free, his sound mind returned. When the villagers arrived, they were greatly surprised to find the clothed man hearing the teachings of Jesus. Unfortunately, they were distraught over losing their herd of swine upon which the demons entered- after all, they failed to understand that this man was more valuable than thousands of swine and all the riches of the world. They beseeched Jesus to depart from their shore. But the man, now devoid of the legion of demons, requested Jesus to permit him to follow the Lord. But Jesus told him: *Go home to thy friends, and tell them how great things the Lord hath done for thee, and hath had compassion on thee* (Mark 5:19). In the above case, as a result of being possessed by the numerous demons, the man had lost his sound mind, was dwelling in uninhabited places and tombs, and was constantly tormented by the demons.

Another type of demonic possession is described in the gospel according to St Mark. A man came running to Jesus and said: *Master, I have brought unto thee my son, which hath a dumb spirit; And wheresoever he taketh him, he teareth him: and he foameth, and gnasheth with his teeth, and pineth, away: and I spake to thy disciples that they cast him out; and they could not* (Mark 9:17-18). It turned out that the man's son had been tormented by the demon since childhood. Often it used to cast him into the fire and into the water to destroy him. After Jesus rebuked the evil spirit, it left the boy screaming after casting him down as though dead. Jesus raised him up and gave the fully delivered boy back to his father. In another incident, Lord Jesus delivered a man possessed with a blind and dumb spirit. When the evil spirit left him, the man could see and speak (Luke 12:23). Subsequently, in the next chapter, we read about the deliverance of a woman who had a spirit of infirmity for eighteen years resulting in her bowed together and unable to lift up herself: *when Jesus saw her, he called her to him, and said unto her, Woman, thou art loosed from thine infirmity. And he laid his hands on her: and immediately she was made straight, and glorified God* (Luke 13:12-13). This physical infirmity and crippling was caused by a type of demons.

Several other types of demons were cast out by Jesus during his public ministry, as recorded in the four gospels. Jesus once said: *The thief cometh not, but for to steal, and to kill, and to destroy: I am come that they might have life, and that they might have it more abundantly. I am the good shepherd: the good shepherd giveth his life for the sheep* (John 10:10- 11). Jesus healed the sick, the blind, the deaf, the dumb, the maimed, the crippled, and all those who were afflicted by demons in various ways.

It is quite likely that modern theologians may consider demonic possessions to be various categories of mental diseases, and thus seek scientific explanations for these afflictions. It is only when they come across demonic oppression or possession in real life that they realise the existence of demons and the veracity of all things written in the Bible.

Two intellectual pastors, of my acquaintance, in their Sunday sermons voiced that demons are the personifications of evil as a result of man's rampant imaginations. One of them even stated that the man possessed with a legion of demons, on the shores of Gadarenes, suffered an extreme case of schizophrenia or split personality- although he did not provide any explanation for the herd of swine plunging themselves into the sea. But God's wrath came upon him unawares: within weeks, he became what he preached. The other pastor also suffered a lot as a result of demonic oppression in the family. I apologise for mentioning these incidents, which, unfortunately, are just two examples of many more. But these were mentioned so that others may not commit the same sin. Blasphemy is the worst sin of all.

Some may ask whether demons can cause diverse sicknesses. The answer is Yes. Although most of the sicknesses are caused by pathogenic organisms, unhealthy habits, and sinful lives, demons can also cause similar diseases. Many medical missionaries, who served in Africa and Asia, reported strange diseases with ever changing symptoms under the spell of witchcraft. Even today, worship of Satan, witchcraft, and necromancy are flourishing in several parts of the world, including in the seemingly economically developed and literate countries. But one fact is so sure and certain: no demon can stand before Jesus Christ or his anointed servants.

I have witnessed, first hand, mighty healing miracles and mass deliverance from demonic oppressions during the crusades of Oral Roberts, D.G.S Dhinakaran, Paul Dhinakaran, David Terrel, Richard Roberts, and many other servants of God, held in Trivandrum. We are thrilled to read about the mighty miracles which Jesus performed during his public ministry and those which the apostles did in the first century AD. Every day, Jesus would have healed and delivered thousands of people afflicted with demonic bondages and various sicknesses, although only a few examples are recorded in the gospels. Moreover, none remained unhealed and disappointed after meeting Jesus during his public ministry. And I found a certain Hollywood movie to be unbiblical and blasphemous, particularly the part in which a paralysed girl was singing praises of Jesus, for even though she was not healed of her physical sickness, her heart was filled with joy and peace after meeting him.

Some years ago, I happened to hear the testimony of a young woman at the Church Renewal Meetings held in Trivandrum. This music student, at the reputed Swati Tirunal Music Academy of Trivandrum, had been left crippled by polio since her childhood resulting in entwined legs which made walking quite impossible, even with crutches. After recognising her musical talent, her parents sent her to the Music Academy to learn Indian classical music. At that time, a servant of God was conducting a healing crusade in Trivandrum. Upon hearing this, her Christian friends encouraged her to attend the meetings and they themselves conveyed her to the meeting ground. On that night, the preacher suddenly announced, by the power of the Holy Spirit, that Jesus was walking in the midst of the crowd and was healing all those who were crippled. Even though Mary had neither the faith for a healing miracle nor the hope for a good future, her Christian friends encouraged her to exercise her faith and to try walking. Lo! The miracle happened! An inexplicable power, as though a lightning, passed through her body and she began to shake violently. In a sudden movement, her legs became straight and normal and she began to walk, praising Lord Jesus Christ who had compassion on her and healed her. She added, in her testimony, that at the same moment, she solemnly pledged that she would sing only for Jesus and not for the world. Jesus honoured her pledge and she became a famous Christian music singer. Lord also blessed her with a family. That is the power of Almighty Jesus who is still doing millions of healing miracles everyday around the world!

I have had the privilege of attending many healing crusades conducted by great servants of God and, consequently, witnessed how blind eyes were opened, how crippled legs were straightened, and how tumours vanished in split seconds. And being a rational scientist myself, I find these to be beyond scientific explanations. But miracles are miracles!

I have heard 'highly spiritual Christians' erroneously saying that miracles happen only to non-Christians and immature Christians, since the mature Christians believe in Jesus and, hence, there is no necessity for convincing them of the miracle-working power of Christ! What did Jesus answer to the woman of Canaan who begged him to deliver her daughter from demonic bondage?- *It is not meet to take the children's bread, and to cast it to dogs* (Matthew 15:26). This essentially means that healing is the bread of God's children. It was only when the woman humbled herself and pleaded, *Truth, Lord: yet the dogs eat of the crumbs which fall from their masters' table,* that Jesus appreciated her faith and delivered her daughter by his word. So my dear brothers and sisters, please remember that divine healing is primarily meant for the children of God. Hence, ask the Lord and receive this.

There are also those who say: "Of course, Jesus did heal the sick, delivered the demon possessed, and raised the dead. And, of course, his disciples did the same too. But the age of divine healings was over by the first century A.D and all prophecies were over after the writing of the book of Revelations in the New Testament." Such individuals are quick to label as heretics those who say "Jesus heals you right now" or if they say some prophecy. If a child of God performs a miracle in Jesus' name or says some prophecy, the aforementioned individuals say that this is done with the help of some evil spirits or with the power of Satan. Interestingly, such blind Pharisees were also there causing hindrances to the ministry of Jesus Christ, two thousand years ago: *they said, This fellow doth not cast out devils, but by Beelzebub the prince of the devils. And Jesus knew their thoughts, and said unto them, Every kingdom divided against itself is brought to desolation; and every city or house divided against itself shall not stand: And if Satan cast out Satan, he is divided against himself; how shall then his kingdom stand? And if I by Beelzebub cast out devils, by whom do your children cast them out? therefore they shall be your judges. But if I cast out devils by the Spirit of God, then the kingdom of God is come unto you. Or else how can one enter into a strong man's house, and spoil his goods, except he first bind the strong man? and then he will spoil his house. He that is not with me is against me; and he that gathereth not with me scattereth abroad. Wherefore I say unto you, All manner of sin and blasphemy shall be forgiven unto men: but the blasphemy against the Holy Ghost shall not be forgiven unto men. And whosoever speaketh a word against the Son of man, it shall be forgiven him: but whosoever speaketh against the Holy Ghost, it shall not be forgiven him, neither in this world, neither in the world to come* (Matthew 12:24-32). From this passage, it can be easily comprehended that the modern versions of the blind Pharisees are committing such a grievous sin, whether it be knowingly or unknowingly!

Then there are individuals who believe that God should not be hassled by us with our petty prayers for the sick, for they consider sickness as a means for the chastisement of God's children. Quoting Hebrews 12:6 (*For whom the Lord loveth he chasteneth, and scourgeth every son whom he receiveth*), they encourage people to suffer. Admittedly, these proponents are often found frantically searching for medical treatments and spiritual treatments (in the form of prayer and miracles) when they are besieged by sufferings or sicknesses.

There are also those who argue that since the Lord did not heal St.Paul of his infirmity in his flesh, in spite of his fervent prayers thrice (II Corinthians 12:7-9), it is the will of God that we too should suffer sickness in our bodies and should not pray for healing. Let us examine these very words of St.Paul: *And lest I should be exalted above measure through the abundance of the revelations, there was given to me a thorn in the flesh, the messenger of Satan to buffet me, lest I should be exalted above measure. For this thing I besought the Lord thrice, that it might depart from me. And he said unto me, My grace is sufficient for thee: for my strength is made perfect in weakness. Most gladly therefore will I rather glory in my infirmities, that the power of Christ may rest upon me* (II Corinthians 12:7-9). Evidently, St Paul specifies lest he should be exalted above measure through the abundance of revelations Lord permitted him to carry this infirmity in his body. It is emphatically confirmed by the repetition of the phrase "lest I should be exalted above measure" in the same verse (II Corinthians 12:7). In his book "Ever Increasing Faith"[14], Smith Wigglesworth mentions visiting a patient who held the notion that her sickness was similar to the thorn given to St.Paul. Wigglesworth asked her, "Are you so saintly and abundant in spiritual life as St.Paul? You sinner, repent and confess your sins." Immediately she broke down and confessed her sins, and was immediately healed by our gracious Lord.

When I sat down to write this chapter, I never intended to cite the aforementioned examples. But the Holy Spirit led me to write these so that those who have such preset notions and prejudices can discard these, humble themselves before the throne of grace, and ask (in childlike faith) Jesus Christ, the Lord who heals, for miraculous healing and deliverance for them or for their loved ones.

---

[14] Wigglesworth, Smith. The Teachings of Smith Wigglesworth: Ever Increasing Faith and Faith That Prevails. 1924. Reprint, Radford, VA: Wilder Publications, 2007.

Hebrews 13:8 proclaims: *Jesus Christ the same yesterday, and today, and for ever.* Accordingly, Jesus Christ, who did mighty healing miracles during his public ministry, has been conducting the same ministry through the apostles (in the first century) and through his anointed servants (all through these centuries). He is doing the same even today and will do so until his second coming. He is the Alpha and the Omega. He is the eternal God. Jesus Christ not only heals physical ailments and sicknesses but also mental and spiritual infirmities. He heals broken relationships, broken families, broken congregations, and the broken world mutilated by man's atrocities. He restores peace, health, prosperity, and harmony in the universe. However, the greatest event of healing miracles is yet to happen - for this will occur at the time of his second coming as explained in the 35th chapter of Isaiah: *The wilderness and the solitary place shall be glad for them; and the desert shall rejoice, and blossom as the rose. It shall blossom abundantly, and rejoice even with joy and singing: the glory of Lebanon shall be given unto it, the excellency of Carmel and Sharon, they shall see the glory of the LORD, and the excellency of our God. Strengthen ye the weak hands, and confirm the feeble knees. Say to them that are of a fearful heart, Be strong, fear not: behold, your God will come with vengeance, even God with a recompense; he will come and save you. Then the eyes of the blind shall be opened, and the ears of the deaf shall be unstopped. Then shall the lame man leap as an hart, and the tongue of the dumb sing: for in the wilderness shall waters break out, and streams in the desert. And the parched ground shall become a pool, and the thirsty land springs of water: in the habitation of dragons, where each lay, shall be grass with reeds and rushes. And an highway shall be there and a way, and it shall be called The way of holiness; the unclean shall not pass over it; but it shall be for those: the wayfaring men, though fools, shall not err therein. No lion shall be there, nor any ravenous beast shall go up thereon, it shall not be found there; but the redeemed shall walk there: And the ransomed of the LORD shall return, and come to Zion with songs and everlasting joy upon their heads: they shall obtain joy and gladness, and sorrow and sighing shall flee away.* In short, the Lord will restore everything to how it was in the Garden of Eden, before the fall of man. Let us look forward to this. Even the very name of Jesus can dispel all our fears and tears. Before his ascension Jesus told his disciples, *And these signs shall follow them that believe; In my name shall they cast out devils; they shall speak with new tongues; They shall take up serpents; and if they drink any deadly thing, it shall not hurt them; they shall lay hands on the sick, and they shall recover* (Mark 16:17-18). This is exactly what the apostles did during the first century A.D, and since then, this ministry has been continued and is continuing even today all the more.

How sweet the name of Jesus sounds
In a believer's ear;
It soothes his sorrows, heals his wounds,
And drives away his fear.
It makes the wounded spirit whole,
And calms the troubled breast;
'Tis manna to the hungry soul,
And to the weary rest.
Dear Name, the Rock on which I build,
My Shield and Hiding-place,
My never-failing Treasury, filled
With boundless stores of grace.
Jesus, my Shepherd, Saviour, Friend,
My Prophet, Priest, and King,
My Lord, my Life, my Way, my End,
Accept the praise I bring.
(Hymn No: 112, Sacred Songs and Solos[15])

I encourage all those who need healing – physical, mental, spiritual, or social- to join me in the following prayer:

Our gracious Lord Jesus,

Have mercy upon us and hear us when we pray. During your public ministry in the holy land, some two thousand years ago, you were moved with compassion. You touched the lepers <u>and healed them. You touched</u> the blind and gave them sight.

[15] Sankey, I. Sacred Songs and Solos. London: Marshall, Morgan, and Scott, 1981.

You laid your virtuous hand upon the people who had been afflicted with diverse sicknesses and infirmities and healed them all. Even those who touched your garment were healed. You even raised the dead. You sent your word and healed the sick and the demon possessed. We beseech you Lord, to have compassion on the sick and suffering. Lay your nail pierced hand upon everyone; heal them and deliver them. Recompense them with health and gladness for all the days they were afflicted and tormented. Cast out all infirm spirits which bring about sicknesses. Cover every one of us with your precious blood. Let your healing power flow from their heads to toes and grant them perfect healing and joy. We give you all the glory.

In your most precious name we pray, Jesus, and receive healing and salvation.

Amen and Amen.

6
JESUS CHRIST – THE LORD WHO CARES FOR ALL

Are not five sparrows sold for two farthings, and not one of them is forgotten before God? But even the very hairs of your head are all numbered. Fear not therefore: ye are of more value than many sparrows

Luke 12:6-7

Lord Jesus commenced his ministry in the most unexpected way- and it all happened at the marriage feast in Cana of Galilee to which Jesus and his disciples had been invited. The mother of Jesus was also present. When the wine ran out, his mother Mary approached him saying, *They have no wine.* Jesus replied, *Woman, what have I to do with thee? mine hour is not yet come* (John 2:3-4). Yet, his mother directed the servants to do whatever Jesus would ask them to do. There were six huge water pots of stone nearby. *Jesus saith unto them, Fill the waterpots with water. And they filled them up to the brim. And he saith unto them, Draw out now, and bear unto the governor of the feast. And they bare it. When the ruler of the feast had tasted the water that was made wine, and knew not whence it was: (but the servants which drew the water knew;) the governor of the feast called the bridegroom, And saith unto him, Every man at the beginning doth set forth good wine; and when men have well drunk, then that which is worse: but thou hast kept the good wine until now. This beginning of miracles did Jesus in Cana of Galilee, and manifested forth his glory; and this disciples believed on him* (John 2:6-11).

St.Mary has undoubtedly played an important role in Jesus' first miracle. But what I want to emphasise is that Jesus is the Lord who cares for all humans. Imagine the embarrassment and shame which the bridegroom would have felt if there was not sufficient wine for the wedding feast, given that wine is an integral component of the Jewish wedding feast! Evidently, many other guests had not yet partaken in the feast, including Jesus and his disciples. But in order to safeguard the prestige of the bridegroom and to ensure that the feast proceeded unhampered, Jesus performed this miracle out of his concern and love. It is written that his disciples believed on him. In fact, the servants, who took the transformed wine from the water pots, were the first to believe. Neither the ruler of the feast, nor the bridegroom, nor those who enjoyed the new wine were aware that it was Jesus who supplied the new wine. This is a clear example of how Jesus did this miracle not for publicity but to solve a grave crisis and to convince his disciples that he is the eternal provider (Jehovah Jireh).

The chapter 6 of the same gospel relates another miracle which Jesus did with five barley loaves and two small fishes which were meant as the meal of a small lad. *Jesus took the loaves; and when he had given thanks, he distributed to the disciples and the disciples to them that were set down; and likewise the fishes as much as they would. When they were filled, he said unto the disciples, Gather up the fragments that remain, that nothing be lost. Therefore they gathered them together, and filled twelve baskets with the fragments of the five barley loaves which remained, over and above unto them that had eaten* (John 6:11-13). This large multitude comprised of about five thousand men, apart from innumerable women and children. On another occasion, Jesus fed a similar crowd by multiplying seven loaves of bread and a few small fishes, as well recorded in Matthew 15:32-38: *Then Jesus called his disciples unto him, and said, I have compassion on the multitude, because they continue with me now three days, and have nothing to eat: and I will not send them away fasting, lest they faint in the way. And his disciples say unto him, Whence should we have so much bread in the wilderness, as to fill so great a multitude? And Jesus saith unto them, How many loaves have ye? And they said, Seven, and a few little fishes. And he commanded the multitude to sit down on the ground. And he took the seven loaves and the fishes, and gave thanks, and brake them, and gave to his disciples, and the disciples to the multitude. And they did all eat, and were filled: and they took up of the broken meat that was left seven baskets full. And they that did eat were four thousand men, beside women and children.* Jesus' love and compassion is very evident- These miracles were done to feed the hungry believers who had been rapt absorbed in his sermons without realising the passage of time.

Towards the beginning of Jesus' ministry, when people pressed upon him to hear the word of God beside the lake of Genessaret, he saw two ships (fishing boats) moored by the lake. He entered into Simon's ship, asked him to thrust it out a little away from the shore, and taught the people who remained standing on the shore. When the sermon was over, Jesus said unto Simon, *Launch out into the deep, and let down your nets for a draught. And Simon answering said unto him, Master, we have toiled all the night, and have taken nothing: nevertheless at thy word I will let down the net. And when they had this done, they inclosed a great multitude of fishes: and their net brake. And they beckoned unto their partners, which were in the other ship, that they should come and help them. And they came, and filled both the ships, so that they began to sink* (Luke 5:4-7). Even though Simon and his fellow fishermen had toiled all night, they had caught nothing. Despite Simon being an experienced fisherman, he did not scoff at Jesus' directions. He obeyed him and got a miraculous catch of fishes. Even at the very beginning, Jesus understood the utter disappointment and anguish in the minds of these fishermen (for their attempts on the previous night was absolutely futile) who were washing their nets for next day's catch. Hence, he not only wanted to grant them a good catch of fishes, but also wanted Simon and his colleagues to leave their fishing occupation and follow him so as to become fishers of men for the kingdom of God. Noted servant of God, Oral Roberts, once wrote to me: "We are dealing with the same Jesus today – the one who scooped out the bed for the Ocean, who flung the stars from His finger tips, who hung the earth on nothing, and who put the fish in the sea. And I'm standing with you in faith believing for your situation to turn around and became great miracle, in Jesus' Name."

The fact is that God cares for each one of us. He cares even for the minutest organism on this planet by providing all factors required for its life.

The first two chapters of Genesis provide an account of the creation by God. Psalm 104 elaborates on God's wonderful creation of plants and animals and His provisions for their day-to-day lives. Jesus said during the Sermon on the Mount: *Behold the fowls of the air: for they sow not, neither do they reap, nor gather into barns; yet your heavenly Father feedeth them. Are ye not much better than they? Which of you by taking thought can add one cubit unto his stature? And why take ye thought for raiment? Consider the lilies of the field, how they grow; they toil not, neither do they spin: And yet I say unto you, That even Solomon in all his glory was not arrayed like one of these. Wherefore, if God so clothe the grass of the field, which today is, and to morrow is cast into the oven, shall he not much more clothe you, O ye of little faith?* (Matthew 6:26-30). Truly Jesus not only fed the people with spiritual manna, but also fed them with solid food whenever a necessity arose. It was due to these reasons that the people wanted to crown him as their king. However, this caused Jesus to rebuke them and leave them.

Jesus also knew that proper rest is necessary for human beings. Once, when he and his disciples were overwhelmed by people from dusk to dawn, Jesus, upon realising that his disciples were tired, asked them to depart and take some rest. He then managed the crowd by himself (Mark 6:31). We have such a caring Master!

After feeding the five thousand with five loaves of bread and two small fishes, Jesus sent the multitude away and dispatched his disciples, in a ship, to the other side of the lake. He then, all by himself, went up into a mountain to pray. But when it was evening, the ship carrying the disciples was in the midst of the lake, being tossed by raging waves due to the strong gusts of wind. And in the fourth watch of the night, the disciples saw a form walking on the lake and were troubled. Gripped by fear, they cried out, *It is a spirit!* But it was none other than Jesus who straightaway calmed them saying, *Be of good cheer; it is I; be not afraid* (Matthew 14:23-27). I believe that when Jesus was praying on the mountain, he would have received the vision of the raging storm in the se and the frightened disciples. And he walked on the lake to approach the ship and to calm the disciples. Simon Peter then requested Jesus for the permission to walk on the lake and join him. Jesus bade him to come and Peter walked on the lake... until he noticed, once again, the raging winds and its obvious effect on the lake. Struck by fear, he began to sink and cried out to Jesus to save him. Jesus stretched forth his hand, caught him, brought him into the ship, and the storm immediately ceased. Although Jesus rebuked Peter for doubting, he did not allow him to be drowned by the waves. This is the loving care of Jesus Christ our Lord! Whenever we are tempest tossed, battered, and shattered, with our faith abysmally low, he comes to our rescue, as in the following popular song:

He will never let go my hand
Jesus never let go my hand
Though the storm may come
And the wind may blow
He will never let go my hand

On another occasion, when Jesus and his disciples were travelling by ship, he fell asleep in the rear part of the ship. A great storm arose and the rough waves tossed the ship and soon it was about to sink. The terrified disciples woke Jesus up crying, *Master, carest thou not that we perish? And he arose, and rebuked the wind, and said to the sea, Peace, be still. And the wind ceased, and there was a great calm. And he said unto them, Why are ye so fearful? how is it that ye have no faith?* (Mark 4:35-40). When we ponder more about what happened, it is interesting to note that the disciples asked, *"Master, carest thou not that we perish?"* They were obviously scared that they would all die and doubted the affection of the one who cared for them the most! How would have Jesus felt, who once told his disciples and the multitudes: *Are not five sparrows sold for two farthings, and not one of them is forgotten before God? But even the very hairs of your head are all numbered. Fear not therefore: ye are of more value than many sparrows* (Luke 12:6-7).

Jesus' love and concern encompassed even those whom society had shunned. One good example is his visit to the pool of Bethesda as narrated by St.John: *And a certain man was there, which had an infirmity thirty and eight years. When Jesus saw him lie, and knew that he had been now a long time in that case, he saith unto him, Wilt thou be made whole? The impotent man answered him, Sir, I have no man, when the water is troubled, to put me into the pool: but while I am coming, another steppeth down before me. Jesus saith unto him, Rise, take up thy bed, and walk. And immediately the man was made whole, and took up his bed, and walked: and on the same day was the sabbath* (John 5:5-9). I believe that Jesus went to this place with the sole purpose of healing this very man who was languishing in his sickness for thirty-eight years, with the desperate hope of touching the moving water one day in the future.

Jesus knows all our limitations. His love, compassion, forgiveness, and power are unlimited. He will surely grant us new abundant lives for his glory. Today, millions of people are languishing in demonic bondages, chronic ailments, alcoholism, drug addictions, inexplicable fears, anxieties, and worries. There is hope and deliverance for these sufferers- but only if they call upon Jesus who is the one and only answer to all our problems. He cares for each one of us. And he is *the same yesterday, and today, and for ever* (Hebrews 13:8).

Jairus, the ruler of a Jewish synagogue, frantically approached Jesus. He fell at his feet and besought him saying, *My little daughter lieth at the point of death: I pray thee, come and lay thy hands on her, that she may be healed; and she shall live.* Jesus went with him and was followed by a large multitude. On the way, there was a woman who suffered from a worsening, incessant issue of blood for twelve years. Implicitly trusting that she will be completely healed by touching Jesus' clothes, she covertly touched the garment of Jesus from behind, without anybody noticing. The healing virtue flowed from Jesus and she was healed instantaneously. But Jesus turned back and asked, *Who touched my clothes?... The woman fearing and trembling, knowing what was done in her, came and fell down before him, and told him all the truth. And he said unto her, Daughter, thy faith hath made thee whole; go in peace, and be whole of thy plague.* This is the love and compassion of Jesus Christ! In the meantime, messengers came from Jairus' house and informed him that his daughter had died and there was need to trouble Jesus anymore. But Jesus told Jairus, *Be not afraid, only believe.* When they reached Jairus' house, they heard the great weeping and wailing. But once Jesus entered the house, he cast out all mourners, except the girl's parents and his three disciples (Peter, John, and James), and entered the room where the girl was laid. *And he took the damsel by the hand, and said unto her, Talitha Cumi; which is, being interpreted, Damsel, I say unto thee, arise. And straightway the damsel arose, and walked; for she was of the age of twelve years* (Mark 5:22-43).

On another occasion, Jesus saw the funeral procession of a youth, the only son of a poor widow of Nain. Truly he was broken hearted at the sight of the weeping and wailing widow. He told her, *Weep not. And he came and touched the bier: and they that bare him stood still. And he said, Young man, I say unto thee, Arise. And he that was dead sat up, and began to speak. And he delivered him to his mother* (Luke 7:12-15).

I firmly believe that these three incidents were not at all accidental but providential. Jesus foreknew what he was going to do: this aspect becomes clearer in the raising of Lazarus from the dead. When Lazarus was ill, his sisters had sent word to Jesus who responded, *This sickness is not unto death, but for the glory of God, that the Son of God might be glorified thereby* (John 11:4). And Jesus stayed where he was for another two days, after which he said unto his disciples, *Let us go into Judaea again.* His disciples advised against this since the Jews were seeking to stone him. Then Jesus said, *Our friend Lazarus sleepeth; but I go, that I may awake him out of sleep* (John 11:11). Then said his disciples, *Lord, if he sleep, he shall do well...* Then said Jesus unto them plainly, *Lazarus is dead. And I am glad for your sakes that I was not there, to the intent ye may believe; nevertheless let us go unto him* (John 11:6-15). By the time Jesus came to Bethany, Lazarus' hometown, it was already four days since Lazarus was laid in the tomb. When Lazarus' sister Martha heard that Jesus was coming, she ran up to him and met him, saying, *Lord, if thou hadst been here, my brother had not died. But I know, that even now, whatever thou wilt ask of God, God will give it thee. Jesus saith unto her, Thy brother shall rise again. Martha saith unto him, I know that he shall rise again in the resurrection at the last day. Jesus said unto her, I am the resurrection, and the life: he that believeth in me, though he were dead, yet shall he live: And whosoever liveth and believeth in me shall never die. Believest thou this? She saith unto him, Yea, Lord: I believe that thou art the Christ, the Son of God, which should come into the world* (John 11:21-27). Then Martha went back to her sister Mary and told her that Jesus had come. Upon hearing this, Mary rose up quickly and came to Jesus, followed by the Jews who were in the house. As soon as she saw Jesus, she fell at his feet, and said: *Lord, if thou hadst been here, my brother had not died. When Jesus therefore saw her weeping, and the Jews also weeping which came with her, he groaned in the spirit, and was troubled, And said, Where have ye laid him?... Jesus wept* (John 11:32-35). Those two words are the shortest sentence and verse in the Bible- one in which the humane nature of Jesus Christ, the Son of God, is well condensed. Many may ask why Jesus wept. Those who saw this exclaimed, *Behold how he loved him!* And some of them said, *Could not this man, which opened the eyes of the blind, have caused that even this man should not have died?* (John 11:36-37). It is true that Jesus loved Lazarus very much. But he also knew that he was going to raise him up from the dead the very next moment. Then what led him to weep? I believe that Jesus saw the agony of bereavement of not just Lazarus' family, but of thousands of families of all times- the past, the present, and the future. When he took up their agonies and sorrows, he was overwhelmed with feelings and broke out into tears (Isaiah 53:4). Then Jesus commands the people to remove the stone, placed at the mouth of the cavernous tomb, despite Martha protesting that the corpse of Lazarus would be stinking since he had been dead for four days. When they took away the stone, *Jesus lifted up his eyes, and said, Father, I thank thee that thou hast heard me. And I knew that thou hearest me always: but because of the people which stand by I said it, that they may believe that thou hast sent me. And when he thus had spoken, he cried with a loud voice, Lazarus, come forth. And he that was dead came forth, bound hand and foot with graveclothes: and his face was bound about with a napkin. Jesus saith unto them, Loose him, and let him go. Then many of the Jews which came to Mary, and had seen the things which Jesus did, believed on him* (John 11:39-45).

Napoleon Bonaparte, who shook the whole of Europe two centuries ago, famously said, 'Impossible n'est pas français'[16]. He was so much confident that he would always be the victor. But alas! Defeated by the British, Napolean was exiled and died humiliatingly. That is the word of man. However, with God, nothing is impossible. The dictionary of God contains no word called 'impossible'. In Genesis 18:14, God asks Sarah, "*Is any thing too hard for the Lord?* This is repeated in Jeremiah 32:27, where God asks the prophet, *Behold, I am the LORD, the God of all flesh: is there any thing too hard for me?* In Luke 1:37, the Archangel Gabriel tells Virgin Mary, *For with God nothing shall be impossible.* Jesus himself has said... *with God all things are possible.* Let us look upon him for a miracle.

The gospel accounts provide only some miniscule glimpses of the manifestation of the care and concern of Jesus Christ for the sick and the suffering. If I quote even these few listed in the gospels, this chapter will become too unwieldy. Yet, let me just mention a few:

[16] (translation) Impossible is not French

When the Samaritan woman came to Jacob's Well to fetch water, Jesus could have simply ignored her given that Jews used to look down upon the Samaritans. But he asked for water so as to enter into a dialogue which not only led to her conversion, but also the conversion of that Samaritan village (John 4:5-42). He also broke down the wall of separation between the Jews and Samaritans. Through the parable of the Good Samaritan (Luke 10:30-37), Jesus taught the Jews that the Samaritans were their true neighbours and friend-in-need. He was so much magnanimous to take them into his sheephold, just as he has included us as well. It is a pity that racial and denominational prejudices still prevail among Christians. St Paul writes: *There is one body, and one Spirit, even as ye are called in one hope of your calling; One Lord, one faith, one baptism, One God and Father of all, who is above all, and through all, and in you all. But unto every one of us is given grace according to the measure of the gift of Christ* (Ephesians 4:4-7).

Jesus also spoke to the Greeks when they eagerly came to hear his discourses. To them spoke he words of wisdom, knowing their love of deep philosophy: *Verily, verily, I say unto you, Except a corn of wheat fall into the ground and die, it abideth alone: but if it die, it bringeth forth much fruit. He that loveth his life shall lose it; and he that hateth his life in this world shall keep it unto life eternal. If any man serve me, let him follow me; and where I am, there shall also my servant be: if any man serve me, him will my Father honour* (John 12:24-26).

Jesus also cared for the little children who were brought unto him to be blessed by him. When his disciples prevented them, they were admonished: *Suffer the little children to come unto me, and forbid them not: for of such is the kingdom of God. Verily I say unto you, Whosoever shall not receive the kingdom of God as a little child, he shall not enter therein. And he took them up in his arms, put his hands upon them, and blessed them* (Mark 10:13-16).

Jesus also went in search of the social outcasts. He healed the lepers.

He called Matthew, the tax collector, to follow him and made him one of his twelve disciples. One day, when the publicans and sinners came unto Jesus to hear him, the Pharisees and Scribes murmured, saying, *This man receiveth sinners, and eateth with them.* At this context, Jesus narrated the parable of the lost sheep, the lost silver coin, and the lost son. He added, *Likewise, I say unto you, there is joy in the presence of the angels of God over one sinner that repenteth* (Luke 15). Jesus did not condemn the women caught in adultery, but forgave her and told her: *go, and sin no more* (John 8:11).

During his last journey to Jerusalem, when passing through Jericho, Jesus called Zacchaeus by name when the latter hid himself amongst the dense branches of a Sycamore tree to have a good view of Jesus, without himself being noticed by anyone: *Zacchaeus, make haste, and come down; for to day I must abide at thy house. And he made haste, and came down, and received him joyfully…. And Zacchaeus stood, and said unto the Lord; Behold, Lord, the half of my goods I give to the poor; and if I have taken any thing from any man by false accusation, I restore him fourfold. Jesus said unto him, This day is salvation come to this house; forsomuch as he also is a son of Abraham. For the Son of man is come to seek and to save that which was lost* (Luke 19:2-10).

When Jesus and his disciples were travelling from Jericho to Jerusalem, Bartimaeus, a man born blind, cried out: *Jesus, thou son of David, have mercy on me.* Those around him rebuked him and told him to be silent. But Bartimaeus cried out louder and louder: *Thou son of David, have mercy on me.* How did Jesus react? *And Jesus stood still, and commanded him to be called* (Mark 10:46-49). Yes, Bartimaeus's cry stopped Jesus Christ even when he was going hastily to Jerusalem to face the sufferings and the painful crucifixion. Bartimaeus, in his joy, cast away his garments, arose, and came to Jesus who asked him, *What wilt thou that I should do unto thee? The blind man said unto him, Lord, that I might receive my sight. And Jesus said unto him, Go thy way; thy faith hath made thee whole. And immediately he received his sight, and followed Jesus in the way* (Mark 10:50-52).

The cleansing of the temple of Jerusalem was a great task which Jesus accomplished, for none would have dared fearing the priests and the Pharisees. He did this for the sake of his Father, for the temple should be a place of solemn worship and not a place of merchandise. Those who did business in the temple were making criminal profits by exploiting the common man. Jesus said: *It is written, My house is the house of prayer: but ye have made it a den of thieves* (Luke 19:46). In the temple, he taught the people, who thronged about him, the parables on the kingdom of God as well as things concerning his second coming and the end of the world. Even though he toughly dealt with the Pharisees and Sadducees, he was considerate and compassionate to the sick and the needy, and healed and comforted them.

Further, we find that Jesus arranged the Passover, which he was to celebrate with his disciples, in a different manner. After the feast, when Judas Iscariot had left, Jesus gave his crucial advice to the eleven disciples (as described in 14th, 15th, and 16th chapters in the gospel according to St.John). He assured them of the baptism of the Holy Spirit and of his second coming, after preparing a place for them in heaven. Then in chapter 17th, Jesus prays the prayer of the Great High Priest unto the heavenly Father for the eleven disciples, as well as for those who would hear and believe their testimonies. Then only does he go with them to the garden beside the brook of Cedron to accomplish his greatest mission- to suffer and to die on the cross. Even there, he lets his disciples go unharmed. He takes the ear of Malchus (cut off by Peter), the high priest's servant who came along with the mob and soldiers to arrest him, places it in its original site and heals him (John 18).

In Luke 23:27-31, Jesus comforts and consoles the women who were lamenting over him as he was carrying the heavy cross amidst cruel tortures and mocking. He turned to them and said, *Daughters of Jerusalem, weep not for me, but weep for yourselves, and for your children. For, behold, the days are coming, in the which they shall say, Blessed are the barren, and the wombs that never bare, and the paps which never gave suck. Then shall they begin to say to the mountains, Fall on us; and to the hills, Cover us. For if they do these things in a green tree, what shall be done in the dry?* In fact, Jesus was foretelling about the persecutions, wars, and tribulations which were to happen in Jerusalem.

Even when he was nailed up on the cross, between the crosses of two condemned thieves, Jesus raised his voice and prayed to God: *Father, forgive them; for they know not what they do* (Luke 23:34). I strongly believe that it is only because of this appeal of forgiveness that the Jewish race survives despite all the great tribulations which they had to undergo. In spite of the unbearable agony, pain, and cruel mockery which Jesus experienced on the cross, he was gracious enough to hear the appeal from one of the two thieves, who were also crucified alongside him, and to grant him salvation. Jesus said unto him, *Verily I say unto thee, Today shalt thou be with me in paradise* (Luke 23:43). When he saw his mother and his beloved disciple John standing below his cross in utter disappointment and anguish, he told his mother, *Woman, behold thy son! Then saith he to the disciple, Behold thy mother!* (John 19:26-27). Thus he entrusted his beloved mother into the care of his beloved and faithful disciple who, *from that hour took her into his own home.*

After his victorious and glorious resurrection, Jesus did not ascend at once to heaven, but stayed back for forty days on the earth, appearing to his beloved disciples and believers, to encourage them and to grant them faith, strength, and hope. He comforted Mary Magdalene who went to his empty tomb; he comforted two of his disciples at Emmaus; he comforted his ten disciples who had been in a closed room in Jerusalem fearing the Jews; he appeared, a second time, in the same room to convince doubting Thomas that he had risen from the dead; he appeared unto his disciples who had gone fishing in the sea of Tiberius. Instead of rebuking them for their inconsistency in faith, he lovingly greeted them and gave them his miraculous breakfast. When Simon Peter brought to the shore a net with one hundred and fifty-three large fishes, he and the others were astonished to find fire of coals with fish laid thereon and bread- which were given to them. Jesus also entrusted Simon Peter to take care of the flock of Jesus – the other disciples and the believer.

In the 24th chaper of Luke, as well as in the 1st chapter of the Acts of the Apostles, we read of how Jesus took his eleven disciples and all his believers to Mount of Olives, to convey his final advice and to entrust them with the mission (the Great Commission) before his ascension. On the day of Pentecost, he sent the Holy Spirit upon them to transform them into brave and mighty witnesses, so as to continue and extend his ministry throughout the world with signs and wonders: *And they went forth, and preached every where, the Lord working with them, and confirming the word with signs following. Amen* (Mark 16:20). His presence and power were always with them.

In the Acts of the Apostles, we find Jesus appearing to St.Stephen when he was being stoned to death; we see him appearing unto Saul on the road to Damascus, not just to prevent him from persecuting the believers, but to make him his own disciple. He stood beside St.Paul on several critical occasions to encourage him and protect him. Jesus also appeared unto his beloved disciple, St.John, in the isle of Patmos to cheer him and to entrust him with his messages to the seven churches in Asia. Above all, Jesus revealed him all things yet to come, as recorded in the book of Revelation.

In addition to all these recorded in the Bible, Jesus Christ has always been, and will always be, with his children in all situations, to protect, heal, encourage, empower, and bless them even unto the end of the world. His unchanging promise is, *and, lo, I am with you alway, even unto the end of the world* (Matthew 28:20). What a caring Lord we have! He will never leave us, nor forsake us.

> *What a friend we have in Jesus,*
> *All our sins and griefs to bear!*
> *What a privilege to carry*
> *Everything to God in prayer!*
> *Oh, what peace we often forfeit,*
> *Oh, what needless pain we bear-*
> *All because we do not carry*
> *Everything to God in prayer!*
>
> *Have we trials and temptations?*
> *Is there trouble anywhere?*
> *We should never be discouraged-*
> *Take it to the Lord in prayer.*
> *Can we find a friend so faithful,*
> *Who will all our sorrows share?*
> *Jesus knows our every weakness;*
> *Take it to the Lord in prayer.*
>
> *Are we weak and heavy-laden,*
> *Cumbered with a load of care?*
> *Precious Saviour, still our refuge-*
> *Take it to the Lord in prayer.*
> *Do thy friends despise, forsake thee?*
> *Take it to the Lord in prayer!*
> *In His arms He'll take and shield thee,*
> *Thou wilt find a solace there.*
> (Hymn No: 319, Sacred Songs and Solos[17]).

Shall we pray together?

---

[17] Sankey, I. Sacred Songs and Solos. London: Marshall, Morgan, and Scott, 1981.

Our gracious Lord Jesus,

The Bible tells us that you love us and care for us infinitely more than our own parents and family. Yet, during several crises, we lose our faith and hope. Often we lament as the heathen do. Forgive us our shortcomings. Forgive our murmurings against you. Forgive our inconsistency in faith and hope. Help us to seek your face always. Help us to pray to you with childlike faith. You know our needs even before we ask. We know that you graciously provide us with everything we need in our lives. Thank you for all the material and spiritual blessings which you have showered upon us. Help us to understand your loving care for us. Protect every one of us, and our beloved ones, from all harm and danger. Provide everything we essentially require in our lives. Remove every sickness, anxiety, and worry. Fill us, Lord, with your peace and joy. Help us to find the purpose in life. Help us to take the right path. Help us to be useful to our own families, to the church, and to the humanity. Lead us in the right way. Help us to help others with all our hearts and to extend your love and compassion to everybody around us. Let your Holy Spirit rule us and guide us. We ask these things in your most precious name, Jesus,

Amen.

JESUS CHRIST – the LORD and GOD

Wherefore God also hath highly exalted him, and given him a name which is above every name: That at the name of Jesus every knee should bow, of things in heaven, and things in earth, and things under the earth; And that every tongue should confess that Jesus Christ is LORD, to the glory of God the Father

Philippians 2:9-11

"JESUS CHRIST IS THE LORD". That was the creed and slogan of the first century Christians. This was blasphemy to the Jews as they firmly believed (and still believe) that there is no other God except JEHOVAH, who brought them out of the bonded labour in Egypt into the land flowing with milk and honey. To the Romans, Caesar was the only lord. Hence, the Christians were persecuted by Jews and Romans alike. In the epistle to Hebrews we read... *and others were tortured, not accepting deliverance; that they might obtain a better resurrection: And others had trial of cruel mockings and scourgings, yea, moreover of bonds and imprisonment: They were stoned, they were sawn asunder, were tempted, were slain with the sword: they wandered about in sheepskins and goatskins; being destitute, afflicted, tormented; (Of whom the world was not worthy:) they wandered in deserts, and in mountains, and in dens and caves of the earth* (Hebrews 11:35-38).

Starting with the first Christian martyr, St. Stephen, innumerable saints, including most of the Lord's disciples, had to face unbearable tortures and executions for upholding their faith that Jesus Christ is the LORD. When St. Stephen was brought before the Jewish council and was falsely accused of having said that Jesus of Nazareth will destroy Jerusalem and will change the customs which Moses delivered unto them, he was steadfastly looking towards heaven: *And all that sat in the council, looking stedfastly on him, saw his face as it had been the face of an angel* (Acts 6:15) When Stephen was asked to explain his stand by the high priest, he narrated the whole sequence of events, from God's calling of Abraham out of the land of Chaldeans until the crucifixion of Jesus Christ the true Messiah. He further charged them: *Ye stiff necked and uncircumcised in heart and ears, ye do always resist the Holy Ghost: as your fathers did, so do ye. Which of the prophets have not your fathers persecuted? and they have slain them which shewed before of the coming of the Just One; of whom ye have been now the betrayers and murderers: who have received the law by the disposition of angels, and have not kept it. When they heard these things, they were cut to the heart, and they gnashed on him with their teeth. But he, being full of the Holy Ghost, looked up stedfastly into heaven, and saw the glory of God, and Jesus standing on the right hand of God, And said, Behold, I see the heaven opened, and the Son of man standing on the right hand of God* (Acts 7:51-56). They cast him out of the city and St. Stephen called upon Lord to receive his spirit. He knelt down and cried with a loud voice, *Lord, lay not this sin to their charge* (Acts 7: 51-60), while they stoned him to death.

Those who stoned Stephen had entrusted their clothes with a young man named Saul who, consequently, witnessed the death of St. Stephen. But he became more violent against those who followed the teachings of Jesus. After committing countless murders and atrocities against the Christians in Jerusalem, he proceeded to Damascus, entrusted with the task of capturing Christian believers and transporting them to Jerusalem for punishment. When he and his men were near Damascus, there was suddenly a blinding and unexplainable light from the sky. Saul fell down to the ground and heard a voice: *Saul, Saul, why persecutest thou me? And he said, Who art thou, Lord? And the Lord said, I am Jesus whom thou persecutes: it is hard for thee to kick against the pricks. And trembling and astonished Saul said: Lord, what wilt thou have me to do? And the Lord said unto him, Arise, and go into the city, and it shall be told thee what thou must do. And the men which journeyed with him stood speechless, hearing a voice, but seeing no man* (Acts 9:4-7). When Saul arose from the ground, he found himself totally blind and had to be guided to Damascus. Here, Saul, in bitter repentance, prayed for three days without consuming any food or water. Then Lord sent Ananias, a disciple, to him; when Ananias laid his hands upon him and prayed, some scale-like matter dislodged from his eyes and he regained sight. Saul did not think twice: he immediately received baptism in Jesus' name and became a new creation in the Lord, adopting a new name- Paul.

Saul's conversion was a terrible blow to the Jews, but it was a great triumph for the Christian church. Paul soon gained the status of an apostle of Jesus Christ. He travelled throughout Judaea, Galilee, and all neighbouring countries convincing Jews that Jesus, whom they crucified, is truly the Christ and the Lord. The tortures and perils which he faced are beyond description. In his second epistle to Corinthians, he challenges the apostles: *Are they Hebrews? so am I. Are they Israelites? so am I. Are they ministers of Christ? (I speak as a fool) I am more; in labours more abundant, in stripes above measure, in prisons more frequent, in deaths oft. Of the Jews five times received I forty stripes save one. Thrice was I beaten with rods, once was I stoned, thrice I suffered shipwreck, a night and a day I have been in the deep; In journeying often, in perils of waters, in perils of robbers, in perils by mine own countrymen, in perils by the heathen, in perils in the city, in perils in the wilderness, in perils in the sea, in perils among false brethren; In weariness and painfulness, in watchings often, in hunger and thirst, in fastings often, in cold and nakedness. Beside those things that are without, that which cometh upon me daily, the care of all the churches. Who is weak, and I am not weak? who is offended, and I burn not? If I must needs glory, I will glory of the things which concern mine infirmities. The God and Father of our Lord Jesus Christ, which is blessed for evermore, knoweth that I lie not"* (II Corinthians 11:22-31). What made Paul face all these adversities with patience? It is nothing but that momentous encounter he had with the living Jesus on the road to Damascus.

Paul had so many other spiritual experiences. Truly Jesus stood by his side on several perilous situations. He had several occasions in which he proclaimed his testimony before Jewish congregations, Jewish council, kings, Roman governors and, finally, before the Roman emperor himself. Once Festus, the Roman governor who took charge in the place of Felix, brought Paul to the Jewish King Agrippa who was visiting him. When Paul was directed to speak, he addressed Agrippa and clearly presented his former background- that of one of the most zealous Pharisees, absolutely believing in Jewish customs, and hence determined to persecute those who believed in Jesus. He continued: *And I punished them oft in every synagogue, and compelled them to blaspheme; and being exceedingly mad against them, I persecuted them even unto strange cities. Whereupon as I went to Damascus with authority and commission from the chief priests, At midday, O King, I saw in the way a light from heaven, above the brightness of the sun, shining round about me and them which journeyed with me. And when we were all fallen to the earth, I heard a voice speaking unto me, and saying in the Hebrew tongue, Saul, Saul, why persecutest thou me? it is hard for thee to kick against the pricks. And I said, Who art thou, Lord? And he said, I am Jesus whom thou persecutest. But rise, and stand upon thy feet: for I have appeared unto thee for this purpose, to make thee a minister and a witness both of these things which thou hast seen, and of those things in the which I will appear unto thee; Delivering thee from the people, and from the Gentiles, into whom now I send thee, To open their eyes, and to turn them from darkness to light, and from the power of Satan unto God, that they may receive forgiveness of sins, and inheritance among them which are sanctified by faith that is in me. Whereupon, O king Agrippa, I was not disobedient unto the heavenly vision* (Acts 26:11-19).

St.Paul was obedient to that heavenly vision until his very end, martyred in Rome. He led many people to Lord even during his time in Rome. Moreover, some of his epistles, written from Rome to churches abroad, inspired those churches in the 1st century AD and still speaks to each one of us. It was the vision of risen Jesus which transformed Saul the scourge of Christians into Saint Paul.

From the four gospels, we can understand that on the day of his resurrection, Jesus first appeared unto Mary Magdalene (who was weeping beside his empty tomb) and then to Cleopas and his companion (on their way to Emmaus), and to his disciples that very evening. The narration by St. Luke reads as follows: *And they (Cleopas and his companion) rose up the same hour, and returned to Jerusalem, and found the eleven gathered together, and them that were with them, Saying, The Lord is risen indeed, and hath appeared to Simon. And they told what things were done in the way, and how he was known of them in breaking of bread. And as they thus spake, Jesus himself stood in the midst of them, and saith unto them, Peace be unto you. But they were terrified and affrighted, and supposed that they had seen a spirit. And he said unto them, Why are ye troubled? and why do thoughts arise in your hearts? Behold my hands and my feet, that it is I myself: handle me, and see; for a spirit hath not flesh and bones, as ye see me have. And when he had thus spoken, he shewed them his hands and his feet. And while they yet believed not for joy, and wondered, he said unto them, Have ye here any meat? And they gave him a piece of a broiled fish, and of an honeycomb. And he took it, and did eat before them. And he said unto them, These are the words which I spake unto you, while I was yet with you, that all things must be fulfilled, which were written in the law of Moses, and in the prophets, and in the psalms, concerning me. Then opened he their understanding, that they might understand the scriptures, And said unto them, Thus it is written, and thus it behoved Christ to suffer, and to rise from the dead the third day: And that repentance and remission of sins should be preached in his name among all nations, beginning at Jerusalem. And ye are witnesses of these things* (Luke 24:33-48).

One of the greatest attributes of God is that He is immortal. Although Jesus died on the cross and was buried in a tomb, his body did not undergo deterioration. King David prophesied in the Holy Spirit about this: *... my flesh also shall rest in hope. For thou wilt not leave my soul in hell; neither wilt thou suffer thine Holy One to see corruption* (Psalm

16:9-10). His mortal body was transformed into his immortal heavenly body, which is not subjected to laws of nature, and He lives forever and ever as Lord and God.

St. John's gospel states that when Jesus met the disciples in the above-mentioned situation, Thomas, called Didymus, was not present. Thus, when the others told him that they saw the Lord, he did not believe but commented, *Except I shall see in his hands the print of the nails, and put my finger into the print of the nails, and thrust my hand into his side, I will not believe* (John 20:25). And after eight days, when Thomas was also in a closed room with the other disciples, Jesus stood in their midst and said, *Peace be unto you.* Then Jesus said to Thomas, *Reach hither thy finger, and behold my hands; and reach hither thy hand, and thrust it into my side: and be not faithless, but believing. And Thomas answered and said unto him, My Lord and my God. Jesus saith unto him: Thomas, because thou hast seen me, thou hast believed: blessed are they that have not seen, and yet have believed* (John 20:26-29).

It was this Thomas who first brought the glorious gospel of our Lord and Saviour Jesus Christ to the Indian subcontinent. He landed at Crangannore (Kodungalloor), near Cochin, in AD 52, after which he established seven major churches situated in present-day Kerala and one small church in Kanyakumari District of Tamil Nadu state. Then he moved to the east coast of India and established several churches in the present Tamil Nadu, until he died as a martyr at the now St. Thomas Mount near Madras (Chennai) airport. He built the inner chapel of the present day church at the location. It was on that very site that, whilst he was praying, he was stabbed to death in the back by a fanatic native. His body was buried at Mylapore and now his tomb can be found inside the magnificent San Thom Cathedral at Mylapore in Madras. The museum adjacent to the Cathedral maintains ancient relics including the spearhead (which had pierced into his body) and also several ancient inscriptions. What made the doubting Thomas into most ardent believer of Jesus? It was surely his encounter with the risen Jesus. And what made Simon Peter, who thrice denied Jesus on the night of Jesus' betrayal for fear of his life, to proclaim that Jesus is both Christ and the Lord to thousands of people? It was nothing but his several encounters with the risen Lord. And what transformed the timid and frightened disciples to go out and bravely proclaim the gospel despite all persecutions and slaughter? It was nothing but their encounter with the risen Jesus. And what made the first century Christians face tortures and death and yet not even uttering a word against their unlawful persecutors? It was their encounters with the risen Lord and/or the testimonies they heard from the disciples of Jesus. Moreover, some of them, on the day of Pentecost, had received the power of the Holy Spirit.

Nero, the sadistic Roman emperor who found fault with innocent Christians for all his misfortunes, enjoyed watching them being tortured, burnt to death, killed and eaten up by lions, smashed by bulls, to mention a few[18]... He even burnt Rome putting all Christians inside and blocking their means of escape. What happened to Nero? He became mad and committed suicide. The city where Christians were ridiculed, tortured, and brutally murdered over the course of 3 centuries for adhering to their faith became the centre of Christianity from the reign of Emperor Constantine, with the banner bearing the cross of Jesus fluttering in the sky. Do we need any further proof that Jesus Christ is Lord? Throughout the past twenty centuries, several agnostics, materialists, rival religious and political sects, rulers and emperors tried to wipe out the name of Jesus and the Christian Church. Voltaire, the revolutionary writer who induced people of France to overthrow monarchy through a bloody revolution, had vowed to wipe out the name of Jesus and Christian ideas as he thought that it was the Christian religion which made people

---

[18] Refer to the Roman historians, Tacitus and Suetonius, for accounts written by non-Christians:
Tacitus, Cornelius, and Michael Grant. The Annals of Imperial Rome. Revised Edition ed. London: Penguin Books, 1996.
Tranquillus, Gaius Suetonius. Lives of The Twelve Caesars. Ware, Hertfordshire: Wordsworth, 1997.

submissive to their rulers and forced them to suffer all evils. The same press which Voltaire used to print revolutionary literature was utilised to print Bibles! Voltaire's palatial bungalow became the distribution centre of the Geneva Bible Society! Is it not Lord's doing?

A similar miracle happened in Romania more recently: when Rev. Richard Wurmbrand finally went back to his homeland after the establishment of democracy in that country, he was taken to a large secluded campus to open a Bible Society office. To his great surprise, this was being established at the very inhuman prison where he had spent fourteen long years in an underground dungeon for the sake of the gospel of Christ. In this connection, I remember a verse spoken by Jesus: *And whosoever shall fall on this stone* (Jesus) *shall be broken: but on whomsoever it shall fall, it will grind him to powder* (Matthew 21:44). Jesus Christ is the Lord. None can prevail against him.

> *Crowns and thrones may perish,*
> *Kingdoms rise and wane,*
> *But the Church of Jesus*
> *Constant will remain;*
> *Gates of hell can never*
> *'Gainst that Church prevail;*
> *We have Christ's own promise,*
> *And that cannot fail.*
> *Onward, Christian soldiers!*
> *Marching as to war*
> *Looking unto Jesus,*
> *Who is gone before.*
> (Hymn No: 706, Sacred Songs & Solos[19])

The blood drops of martyrs have become the fruitful seeds of the Church. In all places where persecutions occurred, the Church grew with greater vigour. Many of you may remember the shocking news about the murder of the Australian missionary, Graham Stewart

---

[19] Sankey, I. Sacred Songs and Solos. London: Marshall, Morgan, and Scott, 1981.

Staines (58) and his two little sons Philip (10) and Timothy (7), all of whom were burnt to death on the night of 22nd January 1999 whilst they were sleeping inside their jeep after conducting a meeting at Manoharpur village in Orissa, India. Staines had been rendering unselfish and sacrificial service among the lepers in Baripada leprosy centre in Orissa for the past thirty years and, apparently, he had no enemies. After this horrendous incident his wife, Gladys, when interviewed by television reporters, said: "I have no vengeance against those people who took away the lives of my husband and children. My prayer is that they too should come to the love of Jesus Christ.[20]" That shows her Christian faith, fortitude, and forgiveness.

Some years ago, when I was attending the Sunday service at Holy Trinity Brompton church at Knightsbridge, London, a missionary narrated a similar incident which happened in Africa. A British medical missionary, who was ministering among the tribes in a remote village in Africa, faced serious threats from the witch doctors who had been exploiting the ignorant people. Even though they prevented the villagers from receiving medical treatment from this missionary, he continued to treat all those who came to him, especially those suffering from malaria and yellow fever. One day, the witch doctors captured him, bound him to their ritual stake, and after performing their rituals, set fire to the stake. But while he was being burnt alive, he prayed: "Lord Jesus, open their eyes to see the truth." The witch doctors and their followers tore away burnt flesh from his body and enjoyed their ritual feast. The news reached the missionary's wife. Obviously, she was utterly shaken. Yet, she went to the spot, collected his bones, and buried them. She was more determined to work among them, risking her own life. Within a few months, the same witch doctors and their followers repented and gave their lives to Jesus; one became a pastor. This missionary lady, along with this pastor and the former witch doctors attended a

[20] Source: Various news items. Also refer to: http://www.lifepositive.com/mind/ethics-and-values/forgiveness/gladys-staines.asp and http://news.bbc.co.uk/2/hi/south_asia/261391.stm

meeting of the World Council of Churches, where the pastor narrated the whole sequence of events, the transformation from cannibalism and witchcraft to Christian love and faith. He lamented that it was only out of ignorance that they sacrificed such a noble man who came to uplift them. This incident happened only a few decades ago.

The Bible describes Jesus Christ as the rose of Sharon and fairest of ten thousands. Unfortunately, most of the paintings depicting fail to bring out the indescribable beauty, grace, elegance, glory, and radiance due to Jesus Christ- after all, most of the paintings must have used human models. St.John saw Jesus face-to-face in the island of Patmos where he had been exiled because of his testimony on the risen Jesus and his gospel. St.John, who had been an inseparable companion of Jesus, even unto crucifixion, became almost dead at the sight of Jesus Christ in his heavenly glory. Let me quote his own words: *I John, who also am your brother, and companion in tribulation, and in the kingdom and patience of Jesus Christ, was in the isle that is called Patmos, for the word of God, and for the testimony of Jesus Christ. I was in the Spirit on the Lord's day, and heard behind me a great voice, as of a trumpet, saying, I am Alpha and Omega, the first and the last: and, What thou seest, write in a book, and send it unto the seven churches which are in Asia; unto Ephesus, and unto Smyrna, and unto Pergamos, and unto Thyatira, and unto Sardis, and unto Philadelphia, and unto Laodicea. And I turned to see the voice that spake with me. And being turned, I saw seven golden candlesticks: And in the midst of the seven candlesticks one like unto the Son of man, clothed with a garment down to the foot, and girt about the paps with a golden girdle. His head and his hairs were white like wool, as white as snow; and his eyes were as a flame of fire; And his feet like unto fine brass, as if they burned in a furnace; and his voice as the sound of many waters. And he had in his righthand seven stars: and out of his mouth went a sharp twoedged sword: and his countenance was as the sun shineth in his strength. And when I saw him, I fell at his feet as dead. And he laid his right hand upon me, saying unto me, Fear not; I am the first and the last: I am he that liveth, and was dead; and, behold, I am alive for evermore, Amen; and have the keys of hell and of death...*(Revelation1:9-18). St.John never died in Patmos; he miraculously came back to the mainland and wrote the messages to the seven churches in Asia Minor. He also wrote the revelations regarding the future events in the world and church histories, as is in the book of Revelation. Many of these events happened in subsequent years and many are yet to happen. Let each one of us read the book of Revelation and prepare ourselves, our families, and our nations for the second coming of our Lord and Saviour Jesus Christ.

In the fourth chapter of the Revelation St.John glimpsed God's heavenly throne and the heavenly worship. In the fifth chapter, he gets a symbolic vision of Jesus Christ, the Lamb of God who takes away the sins of the world, and the praise, worship, and honour which Jesus receives in heaven, as is due. John further writes: *And I beheld, and I heard the voice of many angels round about the throne and the beasts and the elders: and the number of them was ten thousand times ten thousand, and thousands of thousands; Saying with a loud voice, Worthy is the Lamb that was slain to receive power, and riches, and wisdom, and strength, and honour, and glory, and blessing. And every creature which is in heaven, and on the earth, and under the earth, and such as are in the sea, and all that are in them, heard I saying, Blessing, and honour, and glory, and power, be unto him that sitteth upon the throne, and unto the Lamb for ever and ever. And the four beasts said, Amen. And the four and twenty elders fell down and worshipped him that liveth for ever and ever* (Revelation 5:11-13). Other passages in Revelation also describe the lamb and the martyrs who died for him during the years of tribulation. A description of Lord's second coming is provided further on: *And I saw heaven opened, and behold a white horse; and he that sat upon him was called Faithful and True, and in righteousness he doth judge and make war. His eyes were as a flame of fire, and on his head were many crowns; and he had a name written, that no man knew, but he himself. And he was clothed with a vesture dipped in blood: and his name is called The Word of God. And the armies which were in heaven followed him upon white horses, clothed in fine linen, white and clean. And out of his mouth goeth a sharp sword, that with it he should smite the nations: and he shall rule them with a rod of iron: and he treadeth the winepress of the fierceness and wrath of Almighty God. And he hath on his vesture and on his thigh a name written, KING OF KINGS, AND LORD OF LORDS* (Revelation 19:11-16).

Composer Georg Händel's famous oratorio 'Messiah' praises Jesus as the King of Kings and Lord of Lords. Several years ago (and what I deem to be the greatest musical event which I ever witnessed), I attended a grand musical concert of this oratorio jointly conducted by London Symphony Orchestra, New Philharmonic Choir, and several other famous choirs of United Kingdom at the Royal Albert Hall, London. The original music and words of "Messiah" is still exhibited in the British Museum, London, where a brief note states that the best musicians/composers of our time will require at least 29 days to compose and harmonise this masterpiece. Händel claims to have dreamt this in one night; the very next morning, he sat down and wrote this from his memory. I fully believe that this oratorio is a divine revelation of Jesus Christ, starting from the very beginning and culminating in Christ's eternal reign in heaven.

The Golden Gate is the oldest of the gates in Jerusalem's Old City walls. The Jews believe that the Messiah will enter Jerusalem via this gate, which will suddenly open to receive the redeemer of the children of Israel. This is the gate through which Jesus and his disciples entered Jerusalem on Palm Sunday. In AD 1541, this was sealed off by the famous Ottoman Sultan, Suleiman the Magnificent, believing that this action will foil the Messiah from entering Jerusalem! King David sang: *Lift up your heads, O ye gates; and be ye lift up, ye everlasting doors; and the King of glory shall come in. Who is this King of glory? The LORD strong and mighty, the LORD mighty in battle. Lift up your heads O ye gates; even lift them up, ye everlasting doors; and the King of glory shall come in. Who is this King of glory? The LORD of hosts, he is the King of glory* (Psalm 24:7-10). All of these passages clearly illustrate the fact that Jesus Christ of Nazareth, whom the Jews rejected and crucified unlawfully, is the Messiah, the Christ, the King of Kings, LORD of LORDS, the King of glory and Lord of Hosts - all the same individual.

On the day of Pentecost, filled with the Holy Spirit and power from God, Peter declared unto a huge crowd of wonderstruck Jews who had gathered: *This Jesus hath God raised up, whereof we all are witnesses. Therefore being by the right hand of God exalted, and having received of the Father the promise of the Holy Ghost, he hath shed forth this, which ye now see and hear. For David is not ascended into the heavens: but he saith himself, The LORD said unto my Lord, Sit thou on my right hand, Until I make thy foes thy footstool. Therefore, let all the house of Israel know assuredly, that God hath made that same Jesus, whom ye have crucified, both Lord and Christ* (Acts 2:32-36). Ever since then, and until now, several saints had the privilege of seeing the risen Jesus face-to-face and such encounters transformed their lives. They include also those of the twentieth century (e.g.Sadhu Sundar Singh, Smith Wigglesworth, T.L.Osborne, Oral Roberts, D.G.S.Dhinakaran, David Terrell, and so many other men of God and also innumerable ordinary believers) who lead spotless lives and remain always in communion with Jesus Christ.

Some of you may have read the biography of Sadhu Sundar Singh, a saint who literally followed Jesus' teachings and lived a holy and saintly life just as a true disciple of Jesus. He had no belongings, not even extra clothes. He travelled bare-footed, even through the snow-covered Himalayan mountain ranges. This frequently resulted in the wounding and bleeding of his feet and, hence, he was known as the 'Bleeding feet Apostle'. "At the Master's Feet"[21] is, in fact, an account of Sundar Singh's encounters with Jesus- we read of how, akin to a teacher tutoring a willing student, Jesus taught him several Biblical

---

[21] Singh, Sadhu Sundar, Arthur Parker, and Rebecca Parker. At the Master's Feet. London: Fleming H. Revell, 1922.

truths. It is worth relating how Sundar Singh became a servant of God: He was born on 3rd September 1888 at Rampur in Punjab into an influential Sikh family. His mother, hoping to make him a Sikh Guru, provided him with the famous books of Hindu and Sikh religions. Although he studied in a Christian mission school in Rampur, Sundar developed a bitter hatred towards Christians and the Christian faith. He exhibited this by burning the New Testament which he got from the mission school.

Sundar accepted the Lord on 15th December 1904. For the preceding three days, he had confined himself to his room, pondering over what the true religion was and who is the true God- obviously, he found no answer. But on 15th December, he was so restless that he was walking back and forth inside his room. Mrs. Rebecca Parker narrates[22]: *"So one night he made a firm resolve that he would obtain peace before dawn-either in this world or the next. He knew that at five o'clock each morning the Ludhiana express passed at the bottom of his father's garden, and to end his misery seemed no sin to the Hindu boy. In Hindu fashion he bathed, and with Testament in hand he retired to his room to spend the long night in reading, meditation and prayer. Just before dawn Sundar became conscious of a bright cloud filling the room, and in the cloud he saw the radiant figure and face of Christ. As he looked upon the vision it seemed to him that Christ spoke saying, " Why do you oppose Me ? I am your Saviour. I died on the cross for you." His determined enmity was broken down for ever as he looked upon that Face so filled with Divine love and pity, and with conviction came a sublime sense of forgiveness and acceptance with Christ. At that moment there flashed into his heart the great shanti he had sought so long. Rising from his knees the vision faded, but from that hour Christ has remained with him, and shanti has been his dearest possession."*

Sundar accepting the Lord as his Saviour came at a very high price.

---

[22] Parker, Arthur Mrs. Sádhu Sundar Singh: Called of God. New York: Fleming H. Revell Co., 1920. (p.20)

Being fanatic Sikhs, his family could not tolerate his conversion to Christianity. They even poisoned him. But it was only because of God's grace that he survived this and other attempts on his life. He visited my current hometown of Trivandrum, albeit long before I was born. He preached at the pulpit of the Mateer Memorial Church, Trivandrum (where I now attend the Sunday service), and his hosts were the Anglican missionaries, Reverend Parker and his wife (who wrote the most authentic version of his biography)[23]. Whenever I enter the compound of the London Mission and the Mateer Memorial Church in Trivandrum, I remember with reverence that some 75 years ago, Sadhu Sundar Singh, undeniably the greatest Christian saint of India, had preached here.

I personally knew another Christian Sadhu, Sadhu Kishan Singh, who went to be with the Lord recently. He was a close relative of Sundar Singh, also born and brought up in an affluent and Orthodox Sikh family in Rampur. As a youth, he was a terror in his locality, which gave him the nickname of *'Saithan Singh'* (Satan Singh). But, Lord Jesus met him and transformed him into a mighty witness for His glory. Like Sundar Singh, he became a saffron-clad Christian Sadhu and preached the gospel throughout India and abroad bringing so many souls into Lord's fold, despite facing so many challenges, threats, and persecutions.

The above examples emphasise that Jesus Christ is appearing even today before his chosen men and women who have been preordained to be his mighty witnesses in this materialistic world of unbelievers. Bro.D.G.S. Dhinakaran, the founder of Jesus Calls Ministries, had several encounters with risen Jesus which transformed him into a mighty man of God to carry the healing virtue of Jesus with Lord's love and compassion throughout the world.

---

[23] References in previous page.

I may be doing an unpardonable sin before my Lord Jesus if I withhold my own testimony. I am an ordinary man, engaged in scientific research and teaching, not having anything to boast of, either materially or spiritually. But it pleased my Lord to draw me closer and closer to him, from a state of nominal and traditional Christianity to the true Christian faith. But even though my experiences are very meagre when compared to those of others, I am testifying these. Jesus said: *Whosoever therefore shall confess me before men, him will I confess also before my Father which is in heaven. But whosoever shall deny me before men, him will I also deny before my Father which is in heaven* (Matthew 10: 32 - 33).

My first encounter with Jesus was on 7th September 1975, when attending an all-night prayer session conducted by Mrs. Rajamma (a pious Christian lady of Neyyoor). All of a sudden, I heard a majestic masculine voice behind me saying: *Arise shine; for thy light is come.* I looked back and saw no one behind me. On the other hand, I saw a great beam of light coming towards me from the front and entering into my heart. I was filled with peace and joy which could not be described in words. Mrs. Rajamma, who was on the dais, came running towards me and laid her hand upon my head, saying the same words in the vernacular (Tamil) language. Then I realised that it was Jesus who spoke to me in English. From that day onwards until today, the Lord's joy and peace prevail in my heart, even though I had to pass through so many crises in my life.

The second incident was in the first week of January 1981, when Rev.Masillamony, a great revival preacher from Hyderabad, was praying for the baptism of the Holy Spirit during his revival meeting at the Christ Church (C.S.I), Trivandrum. I felt as though a gust of hot air was targeted at me from high.

The third incident was during the Jesus Calls Good News Festival conducted by Dr. D.G.S.Dhinakaran at the Police Stadium, Trivandrum. I was running around since I was in charge of the 350-strong volunteer force to manage the mammoth gathering. On the very first night, when Bro.Dhinakaran made the opening prayer, power fell upon me, enabling me to perform my duties in the best way possible with Lord's strength. For five consecutive evening sermons, Bro.Dhinakaran's key verse was *Come unto me, all ye that labour and are heavy laden, and I will give you rest* (Matthew 11:28). The sermons were saturated with the love and compassion of Jesus. I could feel the Lord's presence everywhere within the stadium. People were shedding tears of repentance and were experiencing physical and spiritual healings. All sorts of sicknesses were healed; cripples were healed, demon-possessed were released from their bondage, cancers were cured, blind eyes were opened, and hundreds were born again. Even though hundreds received the baptism of the Holy Spirit with the sign of tongues, I did not- yet I too received the anointing with power and fire, coupled with unspeakable joy. This very venue had witnessed mighty miracles by Jesus, several years ago, during Bro.Oral Roberts' crusade in 1964. I still remember the thrill upon witnessing a lame man (who used to beg in the city streets) climbing up the steps to the dais and raising his crutches high up in the air. This resulted in a great tumult in the city since none could refute his miraculous healing by Lord Jesus Christ. For several years later, such spectacular miracles did not publicly happen in Trivandrum. Hence, when Bro. Dhinakaran's meetings witnessed more such miracles, the newspapers wrote: "Biblical days are back here in Trivandrum." We give all praise, honour, and glory to Lord Jesus who performed those miracles.

In April 1981, an Anglican charismatic team, under the leadership of Rev.John Wyndham of Australia (who later became the international president of SOMA), conducted church renewal meetings at the Mateer Memorial Church (C.S.I), Trivandrum. When one of the team members, Rev. Harold Clark of New Zealand, placed his hand upon me, I immediately received a new anointing of the Holy Spirit, yet still without the sign of tongues.

Finally, on February 9th 1982, during a prayer session at the Jesus Calls Institute of Evangelism, Madras, the Holy Spirit convicted me of the sin of talking against the speaking of tongues during my youth. When I confessed the sin with a broken heart and bitter tears, mighty power, as though a lightning, fell upon me and opened my lips to praise the Lord in several different tongues and sing in the Spirit. During another prayer session conducted by Bro.Dhinakaran, Lord Jesus stood by my side, his soft woollen garment touching me. When I reached out to touch him, he was around me, as a pillar of fire, filling me with a fiery anointing and with the heavenly bliss. At the conclusion of the evangelists' training programme, when Bro. Dhinakaran laid his hands upon me and prayed, Lord Jesus also filled me with the gifts of the Holy Spirit.

I now believe that all these happened since the Lord's purpose was to use me in the Medical College campus, Trivandrum, in the healing ministry. The horrible plight of patients, especially those afflicted with cancer, broke my heart; every day, I used to tearfully pray: "Lord Jesus, come to the Cancer Hospital just as you went to the pool at Bethesda and heal those who fight for their lives here."

I commenced a special programme of teaching on the ministry of Jesus Christ and the nine gifts of the Holy Spirit to the Christian doctors, medical students, and paramedical staff. Most of them were blessed with the gifts of the Holy Spirit, along with Lord's love and compassion. Thereafter, we used to go and pray for the patients who requested prayer. And our Lord Jesus healed all manner of diseases and sickness, including cancer, myocardial infarction, kidney failure, brain damages, and demonic bondages. We give all glory and honour to Jesus Christ who performed these miracles. Even though many of my colleagues and well-wishers advised me to publish at least a newsletter, I was determined to do this ministry as Jesus did - without any publicity.

One unique incident is worth mentioning: When two of us were praying for a lady who was paralysed (with paraplegia) because of a tumour on her spinal cord, I felt as if someone stood beside me as though to join us in prayer. But suddenly, a mighty power fell upon me and forced me to say, "In the name of Jesus Christ of Nazareth, rise up and walk." Immediately, I eagerly opened my eyes to see who stood next to me and all I could see was a glimpse of the dazzling white robe of Jesus swiftly moving away behind me. We then realised that it was Jesus who stood besides us. The lady got up from the bed totally healed and was discharged from the hospital the very next day! Glory be to Jesus! Most importantly, for the first time, I saw the glory of Jesus with my open eyes even though I could not see him entirely.

On 28th January 1985 another great miracle happened in my life. On that particular day, I got strange skin rashes all over my body. I did not give this much importance, assuming that this was some allergic reaction- until I consulted a doctor two days later and was told that it was chicken pox. This shook me greatly- not because of my sufferings, but because the infection was a threat to my wife and little children. Thus, I adopted a self-declared isolation. I was very disturbed and even asked my Lord, "Why these for me? I cannot go out to do thy ministry at least for a month. And what about my family?" I could neither read my favourite Bible nor pray. But when I rose up to go to the bathroom, I almost fainted and began to fall towards the right. Then, suddenly, an extremely soft hand held my right arm and prevented me from falling. I was shocked- after all, the room was bolted from inside and there was no one else in the room! I looked around to see who touched me. And, in a split second, the hand that strongly held me transformed into a hand of fire and my whole body, from head to toe, appeared to be burnt in fire. My mind became suddenly peaceful. And when I looked at my body, the rashes and pistules had all been burnt out as though roasted on a frying pan! My wife and children could not believe their eyes! We gave thanks and praises to the Lord who came down from heaven and literally touched and healed me instantaneously.

Another supernatural miracle was yet to happen. On 5th March 1985, I was on a nonstop flight of the British Airways from Bombay to London. I was transporting live oral cancer biopsies in an ice bucket, which were to be cultured the same day in a laboratory of the University of Glasgow. Whilst I was reading my pocket Bible, I suddenly heard a majestic masculine voice saying: "Landing at 12 o'clock." Puzzled, I consulted my watch which showed 11 o'clock (Indian Standard Time) and I was quite surprised since the flight was scheduled to reach London only at 4.30 P.M IST. My co-passenger quipped that I must have had a daydream when I queried whether there was any announcement saying "Landing at 12 o' clock." I then realised that it was the voice of Jesus, my Lord, and reasoned that since he said so, this was something which would be accomplished. After a handful of minutes, the Captain announced: "This is your Captain speaking. Because of some technical reasons, we are flying back to Bahrain." I could see the flight engineer rushing towards the cockpit. Then, at exactly 11.15 A.M. IST, the Captain announced: "This is an important announcement. I can no longer conceal the matter. There is a fire in the luggage hold of the plane. I have switched on the automatic fire extinguishers, but that may not be sufficient. We have to land somewhere. I sought permission to land in Turkey. As it was refused, we are going to Bahrain. It will take 45 minutes to reach Bahrain. In the meantime, please obey what my crew members ask you to do."

My readers might be able to picture the situation inside the aircraft: The Jumbo jet was fully packed, with most passengers being British, aged 50 years or more, returning to London from Australia. Perhaps that is why they did not display their inner panic, even though they looked pale and grim. Some of them resorted to praying. My co-passenger, a rich executive from Bombay, was utterly scared. He was astonished at my behaviour, asking me: "Are you not scared? We are going to die in the mid air!" I comforted him saying that we would land at Bahrain safely at 12 o'clock as foretold by Jesus Christ, the controller of the entire universe. And, indeed, at exactly at 12 o'clock, we landed at Bahrain airport. It was only then that the man believed me. The greatest miracle was that even though the plane flew for more than 45 minutes with fire in the luggage hold, yet the fire did not reach the fuel tanks. When landing, the fire and smoke could be seen at the right tail end of the plane but it did not flare up! Soon the fire fighters put out the fire. The captain, who later met us at the Bahrain airport lounge, admitted that it was fairly a big fire and only by God's grace did we survive (the only damages were some baggage and certain parts of the luggage-hold of the aircraft). I shared my testimony with him and a few others who were there. And when I got back my baggage, I found it to be intact, although smoke and soot had tarnished its surface. What a wonderful saviour we have! His name is wonderful!

The past several years have seen innumerable personal experiences in which Lord Jesus helped me in miraculous ways. However, my greatest spiritual experience to date is my encounter with Jesus, vis-à-vis, on the night of 29th January 1984 at Ernakulam, India. This was on the final day of the Jesus Calls Good News Festival and the previous four nights had witnessed mighty miracles which shook the city and the state. So tremendous were these miracles that anti-Christian organisations resorted to printing pamphlets against Jesus Christ and Christian faith. In fact, even we were handed such pamphlets whilst going to the Marine Drive Stadium to attend the evening meeting on the final day! I was very sad upon reading those pamphlets, unable to comprehend why they could not understand the truth when Jesus demonstrated his compassion on the people of that city by healing them. On that night, when Bro.Dhinakaran made an altar call for evangelists and the youth who wanted to dedicate their lives for the ministry of Jesus, hundreds moved towards the open space in front of the dais. As I was in charge of controlling the crowd, I had instructed that only those intending to do Lord's ministry should stand or move. But while the preacher was praying for those who came forward, I saw a man coming towards me from the crowd. I was very angry since this was against my instructions. So, just as I was about to scold him, I truly looked at him and was astonished. It was none other than Jesus Christ, the Son of God, in kingly robes with a golden crown studded with glittering precious stones on his head, a golden sceptre with glittering diamonds on the right hand, and a golden orb on his left hand- I could even see wounds on his head, face, and hands! He had a long golden blond beard and long golden blond hair. Above all, his face was radiant and he looked at me and smiled. His face was in rosy bloom. Truly he is the rose of Sharon and the fairest of all on earth and in heaven. I was so wonder-struck that I could neither move nor utter a word. A peace that passeth all understanding filled my heart; a joy unspeakable filled my mind; a power unparalleled flowed into my being. I gazed, gazed, and was lost in the Lord's unparalleled beauty and grace for a few minutes. Then he vanished. If I were an artist, I would have painted a picture of Jesus as I saw him face-to-face. It almost fits the description conveyed by St John in Revelation. But my greatest surprise is why he met me vis-à-vis when I am still an ordinary sinful man? Perhaps, it would have been to convince me that he is alive and that he is the King of Kings and Lord of Lords even though many may deny his existence and say all sorts of blasphemies against him.

Although I am an ordinary man, Jesus continues to love, guide, heal, and bless my family and me. On 2nd May 1993, I was exploring the rainforests of Ponmudi mountain, some 58 kms from Trivandrum. As I was trekking down from the summit of Ponmudi, my right foot accidentally slipped into a deep crevice in the rock and I almost fell down. I managed to pull out my foot from the crevice but I found that my right ankle was seriously dislocated. My attempts at setting the foot right were futile and my ankle ached much. I somehow limped to the jeep and returned home, where I anointed the aching ankle with several balms and even took some analgesic drugs to alleviate the pain and swelling. But none of these worked and my ankle's condition became worse. I spent a sleepless night, squirming in pain and couldn't wait for dawn (having decided that consulting an orthopaedic surgeon was the only solution). It was about 5 o'clock in the morning on 3rd May when I suddenly felt someone entering my bedroom and sat beside my ailing foot. Within seconds, he caught hold of my aching foot with one hand and the calf with the other hand. Then he pulled out my aching foot a bit and twisted it so that the bones in the ankle were placed in the correct position, as is usually done by an expert in Orthopaedics. I opened my eyes, got up, switched on the light, and looked around to see who it was- but I found none! My wife and children were fast asleep in another room. I looked at my foot. All the swelling and pain had vanished in a split second; peace and joy were restored. Then I understood that it was none other than Jesus Christ our Lord, the greatest physician, who came to me out of his boundless love and compassion and healed me. I presume that since I was intending to consult an Orthopaedics expert to correct my dislocation, Jesus graciously did that very task itself even though a single word from him would have healed me. How much does he understand our thoughts and our situations and comes to our rescue at the right time in the right manner! Lord Jesus is always with me in all circumstances, correcting, guiding, helping, encouraging, and empowering me all the day long even in the midst of trials and hardships. Let us all give all glory and honour due to his most wonderful name.

My dear brothers and sisters in Christ, these narrations were to exemplify the fact that Jesus is risen from the dead and that he is alive for evermore. He is King of Kings and Lord of Lords. He is coming soon to establish his millennial reign on this earth. He is our LORD and our GOD. He alone can save this planet which has been utterly spoiled by man's brutality in the form of wars, riots, violence, immorality, deforestation, environmental pollution, radioactive fallout, etc. Are you prepared to meet him? If not, surrender yourselves fully to him; be born again, be filled with his Spirit, grow from grace to grace and from glory to glory, and earn as many souls as possible for him. May Lord Jesus help you and bless you, Amen.

He is Lord, he is Lord
He has risen from the dead
And he is Lord
Every knee shall bow
Every tongue shall confess
That Jesus Christ is the Lord.

Shall we join in prayer with all our heart and soul?

Lord Jesus Christ,

We thank thee and praise thee from the bottom of our hearts, for forsaking thy heavenly glories to come down to this earth to heal the broken-hearted, to deliver the oppressed, to heal the sick, to deliver the demon possessed, to raise the dead, and to transform sinners into saints. Our hearts overwhelm with gratitude for graciously bearing our sins, sicknesses, and sorrows on thy body, mind, and soul on the cross and for redeeming us by thy precious blood. We rejoice in that thou art risen from the dead and that thou livest forever and ever, ready to help us always. Lord, enable us to have a closer walk with thee; enable us to hear thy voice, enable us to understand thy word as recorded in the Holy Bible; enable us to understand more about thee; enable us to see thee face to face as St. John saw thee in the Isle of Patmos. Fill us Lord with thy power and Holy Spirit. Make us channels of blessings to others. Use us to carry thy gospel far and wide. Help us to do thy will. Help us to be in communion with thee always, until we meet thee at thy second coming.

Amen and Amen

Addendum

I wrote the above testimony in October 2001. Several years have passed since with many episodes of sicknesses, adversities, and stress, and occasional showers of blessings upon my family and me.

I had the privilege of working as one of the chief organisers in conducting the Jesus Calls Trivandrum Prayer Festival from November 8th-11th 2007 at the Police Stadium, Trivandrum; the festival marked the completion of 27 years of Jesus Calls ministry in the city. On 10th November (coincidentally, my birthday), during the prayer session of the evening meeting, Bro.Dhinakaran, being moved by the Holy Spirit, called out and exhorted, "Brother Stephen. God's servant Stephen. Stephen, Jesus tells me once you were used mightily by the Lord. Mighty healing miracles happened in your ministry. But now you are unable to do so because of witchcraft powers working against you and your family. Now Jesus is chasing away those demons and they will never come against you. Moreover, Lord is filling you with tremendous anointing and power. He is giving you back all the gifts of the Holy Spirit and you will be used far and wide, still more mightily in the years to come." In fact, at that very moment, I was anointed with fire and was filled with supernatural peace.

The unexpected home call of Bro.DGS Dhinakaran on 20th February 2008, was a great shock and terrible blow to me as he was my most revered person and mentor on the earth. Nevertheless, the risen Lord Jesus upholds me and guides me even today. Also, Bro. Dhinakaran's family continue to uphold me and my family in their prayers.

I was greatly strengthened, both physically and spiritually, during our

Holy Land pilgrimage in November 2010. I had previously twice tried to visit the Holy Land whilst returning to India from the UK- on both occasions, I could not visit due to the Arab-Israeli conflicts. This time, my daughters arranged the Holy Land tour for the family. We were blessed with marvellous weather throughout our journey. Our pilgrimage commenced from Jordan and the summit of Mount Nebo, from where we saw the picturesque vista of the Holy Land, just as Moses would have seen. We were more excited to enter into the Holy Land and to walk upon the sacred ground upon which our Lord and Saviour Jesus Christ had walked, preached, healed, and performed mighty miracles for the thronging multitudes.

In Israel, our Holy Land experience commenced with a visit to the Franciscan Wedding Church, built on the site of the wedding house in Cana, then the Basilica of the Annunciation, synagogue of Capernaum, Church of Beatitudes, the Church of the Multiplication, Sea of Galilee, the Church of the Primacy of St.Peter, and the mount of the Transfiguration. Although it was a hasty guided tour, we could get glimpses of the historic and archaeological treasures and worship in these sites. We were thrilled to enter into the magnificent Church of the Nativity in Bethlehem, built upon the site of Jesus' birth. Though the crowd was overwhelming, we could descend into and worship at the most holy place where Jesus was born, marked by a fourteen-lobed silver star affixed and also at the crib where infant Jesus was laid. As I climbed up the narrow staircase to come up to the main hall of the church, a dislocation on my right ankle, which persisted for several months, vanished miraculously without even praying for it!

We also visited the Shepherds' Field in Bethlehem where the angel of the Lord gave good tidings of great joy. As the days went on, we were very enriched, especially during our trips to Mount of Olives, the path of Jesus' triumphant entry through the steep slope of Mount of Olives, at the Garden of Gethsemane and the Church of Agony, Court of Caiaphas, Via Dolorosa, Church of the Holy Sepulchre, and the Chapel of the Ascension. We could feel the presence of Jesus and his power in all these holy places. We were blessed to have had the opportunity to pray at the Western Wall, the only remnant of the Temple of Jerusalem. I am certain that the prayers we prayed in those places, not only for us, but also for our loved ones, the church, and the nation of Israel, will never go in vain. It is indeed a great miracle that in spite of several wars, lootings, arson, violence, bloodshed, and earthquakes, these holy places are still preserved. Also the inflow of thousands of pilgrims everyday from all over the world to worship in these holy places reminded me about the prophecies on Jerusalem in the last days. Moreover, the recent developments in the countries around Israel, and global calamities are signs of the second coming of Lord Jesus Christ in glory. Let us prepare ourselves, our families, and churches to meet him. However, please remember the warning given by our Lord: "Nevertheless when the Son of man cometh, shall he find faith on the earth?"

ABOUT THE AUTHOR

Dr.J.Stephen is a well known author in Cell Biology whose name figures in Marquis international "Who's Who in Science and Engineering","Who's Who in in Medicine and Health Care" and "Who's Who in the World". His high position in the scientific field did not deter him from a life fully dedicated to the Gospel of Jesus Christ. His authentic work viz:"Jesus Christ the Lord" is the outcome of his earnest search for the ultimate Truth as revealed in Jesus Christ.

May this great work of this Christian friend clear the doubts in the minds of the earnest seekers and bless them with the knowledge of the real Truth and Life in Jesus Christ.

L.Sam

Dr. Stephen Joshua was born into a strong Christian family in the beautiful village of Cheruvarakonam, Parassala (India), one of the earliest centres of the London Missionary Society in South India. He studied his pre-degree at the Scott Christian College (Nagercoil), followed by a B.Sc and an M.Sc from the University of Kerala (India). He earned a PhD in Genetics from the University of Kerala in 1974. He conducted research as a Commonwealth Fellow at Chester Beatty Research Institute, University of London (1973-1974), where he worked on the cutting-edge cell biology of cancer. A veritable polymath, he had a prolific research career as Professor of Cytogenetics at the University of Kerala and at the Regional Cancer Centre, both in Trivandrum, encompassing several research domains that he was passionate about (including biodiversity, deforestation, and pollution). He published a book on cell biology and several peer-reviewed publications, mainly on cytogenetics, toxicity, cell biology, and cancer. He also engaged in postgraduate teaching, supervised several M.Sc, M.Phil, Ph.D, and M.D. theses, and was a member of international cancer research associations.

He enjoyed gardening, nature, church music, and reading, as well as maintaining several collections. He also loved serving the Lord in all the ways he could. Since his early adult life, he was very involved in church activities, including as a Sunday School teacher, song composer, and a bass vocalist and guitarist in several choirs. He developed a deeper relationship with God in the 1970s (a snapshot of which is provided in his book). From 1980 onwards, he conducted active lay-ministry (in Kerala and Tamil Nadu) as a diligent servant of God, until he went home to be with the Lord on 25 February 2015.

- The Editors

17930956R00073

Printed in Poland
by Amazon Fulfillment
Poland Sp. z o.o., Wrocław